Arduino Programming For Beginners

How to learn and understand Arduino hardware and software as well as the fundamental electronic concepts with this beginner's guide. Getting started Arduino sketches

[Matthew Python]

Legal & Disclaimer

The information contained in this book and its contents is not designed to replace or take the place of any form of medical or professional advice; and is not meant to replace the need for independent medical, financial, legal or other professional advice or services, as may be required. The content and information in this book has been provided for educational and entertainment purposes only.

The content and information contained in this book has been compiled from sources deemed reliable, and it is accurate to the best of the Author's knowledge, information and belief. However, the Author cannot guarantee its accuracy and validity and cannot be held liable for any errors and/or omissions. Further, changes are periodically made to this book as and when needed. Where appropriate and/or necessary, you must consult a professional (including but not limited to your doctor, attorney, financial advisor or such other professional advisor) before using any of the suggested remedies, techniques, or information in this book.

Upon using the contents and information contained in this book, you agree to hold harmless the Author from and against any damages, costs, and expenses, including any legal fees potentially resulting from the application of any of the information provided by this book. This disclaimer applies to any loss, damages or injury caused by the use and application, whether directly or indirectly, of any advice or information presented, whether for breach of contract, tort, negligence, personal injury, criminal intent, or under any other cause of action.

You agree to accept all risks of using the information presented inside this book.

You agree that by continuing to read this book, where appropriate and/or necessary, you shall consult a professional (including but not limited to your doctor, attorney, or financial advisor or such other advisor as needed) before using any of the suggested remedies, techniques, or information in this book.

Table of Contents

INTRODUCTION

When it comes to creating some of your own robotics products, there are many things that you can consider. You will need to decide what kind of project you want to work on as well as the type of code that will help you to get the work done. One of the best options that you can use is the Arduino platform. When we are talking about Arduino, we are talking about a software and microcontroller that is programmable, open sourced, and will use the ATMega chip. It is designed to be more of a prototyping platform, there is a huge fan base for this software when it comes to building an electronic project. When it comes to working with an electronic project, you will find that the Arduino platform is good for using either as a temporary addition while you work on the project or you can even embed it as a permanent part of the robotic project when it is done.

The Arduino board is also programmable with the Arduino software, which is pretty easy to use, even for those who are just getting started and have no idea how to work with this kind of software. If you have happened to use the C + + or Java programming languages, you will see that the Arduino coding language is going to be fairly similar. The idea behind using this software is meant to be really simple, but there is a lot of power there to, making it perfect for those who have some experience and for those who are just getting started out. Arduino is also an open sourced platform, which means that anyone is able to use it, for free, as well as make adjustments to the code to fit their needs. This is a really cool addition for those who are just starting to use the Arduino system because they will be able to access thousands of codes from other programmers, or even make some changes to their own codes, in order to make the program work perfectly. In addition to finding that many of the codes that you would like to use are already available and developed, beginners are going to enjoy that the Arduino community is pretty large. You will be able to go online and look through forums and communities to ask your personal questions related to your own project, to find out new information, and even watch tutorials to make working with Arduino easier than ever. The Arduino platform may be pretty powerful to use, but it is also pretty basic. You will find that this platform only comes with two main components for you to use including: The hardware: this is going to include the microcontroller, which is also known as the circuit board. You are able to physically program this part. You will find that there are a number of Arduino boards for you to choose from and the choice will vary depending on the type of project that you are putting together.

The software: this would be the environment that you use with the board, or the IDE, that is going to run right on your own computer. You will use the IDE to help you to upload and write the programming codes that you would like to be relayed over to the board. Once you write your programs on the board and transfer them over, the Arduino board should act in the manner that you requested.

These parts are able to come together to help you to get the project to work well. You need to make sure that you have some hardware in place, such as one of the Arduino board types, and then it needs to respond to what you are able to send through with the software. We will spend some time talking about the various things that you are able to do with the software in order to get your project to work later on, but both of these will need to be set up to ensure that the messages from the IDE are getting over to the board and working properly. With Arduino, you need to have the IDE in place before writing out any code. The IDE for this program is free since it is open sourced, which makes it easier to get ahold of a copy. When writing codes, you will use the Arduino programming language, which will be easy to learn and works well with all of the operating systems on your computer. One thing to note with the IDE and the coding language with Arduino, if you are working on a Windows 7 operating system or earlier, you will have a few steps that you will need to take, in addition to the regular steps, to make sure that the Arduino board will work with the operating system. It does work with the older versions of Windows, you just need to take some extra time to introduce the board to this system to get it to work. Whether you are just getting started out with programming or want to use some of your skills to make a great electronic or robotic project, the Arduino platform will be able to help you get this done. It has all the power that you need with a simplistic background that helps even the beginner understand and accomplish what they want.

What can I do when using Arduino?

One of the first questions that you may have when you see the Arduino programming language is what you are able to do with it all? There are many programming languages out there and you are able to choose them to accomplish different things, but Arduino is going to work a bit differently compared to some of the others. There are many great projects that you are able to do with the Arduino platform. Basically, the coding that goes with Arduino is going to travel from the IDE on your computer over to the hardware that you purchase to go with your project. You can use just the board or attach it to some electronic project to make it do some amazing things. There are a lot of things that you can do with your robotics with the help of Arduino and if you are just getting started with your own electronic learning process or you want to try something new, this is the best platform to do so with. You are able to work with the board making sounds, blinking lights, sending out signals to control what is on the screen ahead of it, and so many other things. We will spend some time looking at the different projects that you are able to do with Arduino so you get a better idea of what you are able to do with this great language.

Chapter 1:What is Arduino?

History of Arduino

A microcontroller is a small computer board that can be programmed to perform certain functions. At the time, BASIC stamp microcontrollers cost $100 and upward, and, as we will see later, Arduino certainly reduced the costs while maintaining the ability to perform various functions and the ease of programming such functions.

Supervised by Massimo Banzi and Casey Reas, Barragán worked in the computer language called Processing to create the environment, IDE (Arduino's official coding environment and program). He fiddled with the Wiring platform technology to come up with the hardware called ATmega168, the first Arduino microcontroller.

Later in 2003, Massimo Banzi, David Mellis, and David Cuartielles added support for Wiring to their microcontroller board, named ATmega8, and they reworked the Wiring source code, naming it Arduino. Together, the three along with Tom Igoe and Gianluca Martino continued to develop Arduino technologies, and by the year 2013, 700,000 microcontroller boards were sold from the New York City supplier, Adafruit Industries, alone.

After some issues with establishing the trademark for Arduino, which resulted in a split in the company for a few years, Arduino is now a single company that is committed to the development of hardware and software usable by the average person or hobbyist, but also flexible enough to be of interest to the professional engineer.

But what is Arduino?

This history of Arduino might sound as convoluted as the technology itself seems to you. Full of many puzzling and confusing elements, you might feel overwhelmed by the language of "microcontrollers," "environments," and "languages." We will start here, beginning with the definition of Arduino.

How it works is as follows: one purchases the hardware that is appropriate to his or her purposes and then, on a more powerful Windows, Macintosh OSX, or Linux computer, and codes or write instructions for the board and uploads the instructions via a cable. The code is then stored on the microcontroller, and it functions according to the instructions, such as activating a beeping sound when light filters in through an opening door. The light activates a sensor connected to the microcontroller, like an alarm.

In a nutshell, Arduino is an electronic project development platform (or electronic prototyping, as it is also commonly said), consisting of both hardware and software, and which is available under the Creative Commons Attribution-Share-Alike license.

This means that all Arduino project design files are freely available on the internet and that their software is open source. Also, the platform may be used for both personal and business purposes, provided that credits are attributed to the Arduino brand, and project files are also made available under the same license.

The project emerged in Italy in 2015 from a group of developers led by Massimo Banzi. The initial purpose was to create a low-cost, easy-to-work platform that could be used by students to develop their prototypes efficiently and cheaply. It was also thought to assist in the teaching of electronics to art and design students, particularly to create interactive environments, something very much in vogue within contemporary design and arts.

Who Uses Arduino?

A wide array of people uses Arduino for various projects and hobbies, as well as for professional uses. It is known for being simple and straightforward enough for beginners, deep and rich enough for the beginner to grow, and with enough potential for a more advanced user to utilize.

Teachers and students use Arduino, and indeed are the intended consumer base for the products, as Arduino offers a low-cost way to build scientific instruments. This allows teachers and students to practice and demonstrate chemistry and physics principles, as well as get started with programming and building robots.

Designers and architects might use Arduino technologies to build interactive models and prototypes of what they hope to develop on a full-scale. Musicians and artists also use Arduino microcontrollers to experiment with new instruments or techniques in their art.

Just about anyone can use Arduino, including children, that want to start tinkering with coding and computer hardware, as well as hobbyists who simply want to learn a bit about software and microcomputers.

The main reasons for using the Arduino platform in your projects are as follows:

- Low-cost prototyping

- Free simulation software available

- Easy to program

- A large number of tutorials, articles, and projects ready on the internet

- Extensive community of developers and hobbyists

- No experience or extensive prior knowledge of electronics/programming required (however, it is advisable to know the basics at least)

Arduino is not the only electronic prototyping platform on the market. There are other projects and development kits, the most common being Raspberry Pi and BeagleBone. Each uses a different microcontroller and has hardware design with its own characteristics. Prices also vary widely, and some other platforms are not as popular.

The choice of which prototyping kit to use depends on the demands and needs your project imposes. Certainly, given the reasons cited above, Arduino is a strong candidate for most of its projects.

Chapter 2:Understanding of Arduino

Key terms related to Arduino

It will then close a circuit lighting up a bulb as output: a nightlight for your child. On most boards, there will be a Pin LED, associated with a specific pin, like Pin 13 on the Arduino Uno. This Pin LED is the only output possibility built into the board, and it will help you with your first project of a "blink sketch," which will be explained later. The Pin LED is also used for debugging or fixing the code you have written so that it has no mistakes in it. The Power LED is what its name implies: it lights up when the board is receiving power or is "turned on." This can also be helpful in debugging your code. There exists on every board the microcontroller itself, called the ATmega microcontroller, which is the brain of the entire board. It receives your instructions and acts accordingly. Without this, the entire board would have no functionality.

Analog in pins exist on the opposite edge of the board from the digital pins on the Arduino Uno. It is an input into the Arduino system. Analog means that the signal which is input is not constant but instead varies with time, such as audio input. In the example of audio input, the auditory input in a room varies with the people in the room talking and with the noises filtering in from outside the room. GND and 5V pins are used to create additional power of 5V to the circuit and

17

microcontroller. The power connector is most often on the edge of the Arduino board, and it is used to provide power to the microcontroller when it is not plugged into the USB. The USB port can be used as a power source as well, but its main function is to upload, or transfer, your sketch, or set of instructions that you have coded, from your computer to the Arduino. TX and RX LED's are used to indicate that there is a transfer of information occurring. This indication of communication will happen when you upload your sketches from your computer to the Arduino so that they will blink rapidly during the exchange.

Chapter 3: Anatomy of Arduino Board

Now that we know some basics in understanding the Arduino microcontroller boards let us look at the various options you have when purchasing an Arduino board. We will look at price, functionality, amount of memory, and other features to help make your decision as easy and straightforward as possible.

Uno

This is the board in which most people start their Arduino journey. It is on the smaller side in terms of memory but is very flexible in functionality and a great tool for beginners and those wanting to try their hand and mind at Arduino. This model has a mini-USB port which allows you to upload directly to the board without using a breakout board or other extra hardware.

Price: $24.95

Flash Memory: 32kB

SRAM: 2kB

EEPROM: 1kB

Processing Speed: 16MHz

Digital Pins: 14 pins

PWM Pins: 6 pins

Analog In: 6 pins

Operating Power: 5V

Input Power: 7-12V

Leonardo

The Leonardo microcontroller board is functional out-of-the-box: all you need is a micro-USB cable and a computer to get started. In addition, the computer can recognize the Leonardo as a mouse or a keyboard due to its ATmega32U4 processor.

Price: $19.80

Flash Memory: 32kB

SRAM: 2.5kB

EEPROM: 1kB

Processing Speed: 16MHz

Digital Pins: 20 pins

PWM Pins: 7 pins

Analog In: 12 pins

Operating Power: 5V

Input Power: 7-12V

101

This microcontroller contains a lot of features that are not available in other beginner models. For example, you can connect to the board through Bluetooth Low Energy connectivity from your phone. In addition, it comes with an accelerometer and a gyroscope built in to recognize motion in all directions with its six-axis sensitivity. It can recognize gestures as well.

Put together, these features allow you to have motion of or around the device be the input to which the microcontroller will respond with an output.

Price: $30.00

Flash Memory: 196kB

SRAM: 24kB

EEPROM: 0kB

Processing Speed: 32MHz

Digital Pins: 14 pins

PWM Pins: 4 pins

Analog In: 6 pins

Operating Power: 3.3V

Input Power: 7-12V

Esplora

This board is based on the Leonardo but comes with even more technology built into it so that you do not have to learn as much electronics to get up and running.

Instead, you can learn as you see the processes work themselves out.

The input sensors that are built in include a joystick, a slider, a temperature sensor, a microphone, an accelerometer, and a light sensor. It also includes some sound and light outputs. It can expand its capabilities by attaching to other technology called a TFT LCD screen through two Tinker kit input/output connections.

Price: $43.89

Flash Memory:32kB

SRAM: 2.5kB

EEPROM: 1kB

Processing Speed: 16MHz

Digital Pins: n/a

PWM Pins: n/a

Analog In: n/a

Operating Power: 5V

Input Power: 7-12V

Mega 2560

This microcontroller is designed for larger projects like robotics and 3D printers. It has many times the number of digital pins and analog in pins, as well as almost three times the number of PWM pins. This, along with the many times multiplied flash storage, SRAM, and EEPROM allows for projects that require more instructions. There is space for greater complexity and specificity in this Arduino board.

Price: $45.95

Flash Memory: 256kB

SRAM: 8kB

EEPROM: 4kB

Processing Speed: 16MHz

Digital Pins: 54 pins

PWM Pins: 15 pins

Analog In: 16 pins

Operating Power: 5V

Input Power: 7-12V

UART: 4 lines

Zero

This is an extension of the Arduino Uno technologies that were developed. It is a 32-bit extension of Uno, and it increases performance with a vastly increased processing speed, 16 times the amount of SRAM and a many times multiplied flash memory. You will pay for the extensions, at almost twice the price of the Uno, but you much more than double your capabilities with this hardware.

One other advantage of the Zero is that it has a built-in feature called Atmel's Embedded Debugger, abbreviated as EDBG, which helps you debug your code without using extra hardware and thereby increases your efficiency in the software coding.

Price: $42.90

Flash Memory: 256kB

SRAM: 32kB

EEPROM: n/a

Processing Speed: 48MHz

Digital Pins: 14 pins

PWM Pins: 10 pins

Analog In: 6 pins

Analog Out: 1 pin

Operating Power: 3.3V

Input Power: 7-12V

UART: 2 lines

USB port: 2 micro-USB ports

Due

This is a novelty in the microcontroller board world because it is built on a 32-bit ARM core microcontroller, giving it a great deal of power and functionality. It has an extremely quick processor and 4 UART's, giving it a lot of flexibility and availability to perform multiple functions. It is used for larger scale Arduino projects, and while it might not be your first board, you would do well to consider it for any bigger projects you have down the line.

Price: $37.40

Flash Memory: 512kB

SRAM: 96kB

EEPROM: n/a

Processing Speed: 84MHz

Digital Pins: 54 pins

PWM Pins: 12 pins

Analog In: 12 pins

Analog Out: 2 pins

Operating Power: 3.3V

Input Power: 7-12V

UART: 4 lines

USB ports: 2 micro-USB ports

Mega ADK

This is based on the Mega2560 Arduino board, with incredible memory capacity and a lot of availability for input and output. The difference between the Mega2560 and the Mega ADK is that the Mega ADK is compatible specifically with Android technologies, such as Samsung phones and tablets, Asus technologies, and other non-iOS, non-Windows, mobile devices that use Android. It comes at a hefty almost $50 price tag, but if you are looking to incorporate Android into your project, this would be the board with which you would want to do so.

Price: $47.30

Flash Memory: 256kB

SRAM: 8kB

EEPROM: 4kB

Processing Speed: 16MHz

Digital Pins: 54 pins

PWM Pins: 15 pins

Analog In: 16 pins

Operating Power: 5V

Input Power: 7-12V

UART: 4 lines

Arduino Pro (8 MHz)

This is the SparkFun company's take on the ATmega328 board. It is basically the Uno for professionals and is meant to be semi-permanent in installation of an object or technology. The 8MHz version is less powerful than the Uno by half, but it is also a good deal cheaper. It requires more knowledge of hardware to get this one working, as it does not have a USB port or a way to power the board by USB, and thus must have a connection to an FTDI cable or breakout board to communicate with the board and upload sketches. Once you get through the technicalities of getting this board hooked up to your computer, however, it functions like a half-power Uno. Unlike the 16MHz Arduino Pro, this 8MHz Pro can be powered by a lithium battery.

Price: $14.95

Flash Memory: 16kB

SRAM: 1kB

EEPROM: **0.512kB**

Processing Speed: 8MHz

Digital Pins: 14 pins

PWM Pins: 6 pins

Analog In: 6 pins

Operating Power: 3.3V

Input Power: 3.35-12V

UART: 1 line

Arduino Pro (16 MHz)

This is the 16MHz version of the Arduino Pro by SparkFun. It is the same amount of power as the Uno but has the same drawbacks as the 8MHz Pro: you will need to find an FTDI cable or purchase a breakout board from SparkFun in order to make the board compatible with your computer to upload sketches. This means learning a **bit** more about the technology than if you were to start with the Uno, but after getting things set up, this will function the same as the Uno.

Price: $14.95

Flash Memory: 32kB

SRAM: 2kB

EEPROM: 1kB

Processing Speed: 16MHz

Digital Pins: 14 pins

PWM Pins: 6 pins

Analog In: 6 pins

Operating Power: 5V

Input Power: 5-12V

UART: 1 line

Arduino M0

This board is an extension of Arduino Uno, giving the Uno the 32-bit power of an ARM Cortex M0 core. This will not be your first board, but it might be your most exciting project. It will allow a creative mind to develop wearable technology, make objects with high tech automation, create yet-unseen robotics, come up with new ideas for the Internet of Things, or many other fantastic projects. This is a powerful extension of the straightforward technology of the Uno, and thus it has the flexibility to become almost anything you could imagine.

Price: $22.00

Flash Memory: 256 kB

SRAM: 32kB

Processing Speed: 48MHz

Digital Pins: 20 pins

PWM Pins: 12 pins

Analog In: 6 pins

Operating Power: 3.3V

Input Power: 5-15V

Arduino M0 Pro

This is the same extended technology of the Uno as the Arduino M0, but it has the added functionality and capability of debugging its own software with the Atmel's Embedded Debugger (EDBG) integrated into the board itself. This creates an interface with the board in which you can debug, or, in other words, a way to interact with the board where you can find the problems in the code you have provided and fix the issues.

Price: $42.90

Flash Memory: 256 kB

SRAM: 32kB

Processing Speed: 48MHz

Digital Pins: 20 pins

PWM Pins: 12 pins

Analog In: 6 pins

Operating Power: 3.3V

Input Power: 5-15V

Arduino YÚN (based on ATmega32U4)

The Arduino YÚN is a great board to use when connecting to the Internet of Things. It is perfect for if you want to design a device connected to a network, like the Internet or a data network. It has built-in ethernet support, which would give you a wired connection to a network, and Wi-Fi capabilities, allowing you to connect cordlessly to the Internet. The YÚN has a processor that supports Linux code in the operating system, or code language, of Linino OS. This gives it extra power and capabilities but retains the ease of use of Arduino.

Price: $68.20

Flash Memory: 32kB

SRAM: 2.5kB

EEPROM: 1kB

Processing Speed: 16MHz

Digital Pins: 20 pins

PWM Pins: 7 pins

Analog In: 12 pins

Operating Power: 5V

UART: 1 line

Chapter 4: Arduino Family

There are three types of memory in an Arduino system. Memory is the space where information is stored. Flash memory is where the code for the program that you have written is stored. It is also called the "program space," because it is used for the program automatically when you upload it to the Arduino.

This type of memory remains intact when the power is cut off, or when the Arduino is turned off.

SRAM (static random-access memory) is the space used by the sketch or program you have created to create, store, and work with information from the input sources to create an output. This type of storage disappears once the power is turned off. EEPROM is like a tiny a hard-drive that allows the programmer to store information other than the program itself when the Arduino is turned off. There are separate instructions for the EEPROM, for reading,writing, and erasing, as well as other functions. Certain digital pins will be designated as PWM pins, meaning that they can create analog using digital means. Analog, as we remember, means that input (or output) is varied and not constant. Normally, digital pins can only create a constant flow of energy. However, PWM pins can vary the "pulse" of energy between 0 and 5 Volts. Certain tasks that you program can only be carried out by PWM pins.

In addition, in comparing microcontroller boards, you will want to look at clock speed, which is the speed at which the microcontroller operates. The faster the speed, the more responsive it the board will be, but the more battery or energy it will consume as well. UART measures the number of serial communication lines the device can handle. Serial communication lines are lines that transfer data serially, that is, in a line rather than in parallel or simultaneously. It requires much less hardware to process things serially than in parallel.

Some projects will have you connecting devices to the Internet of Things, which essentially describes the interconnectedness of devices, other than desktop and laptop computers, to various networks in order to share information. Everything from smart refrigerators, to smartphones, to smart TV's are connected to the Internet of Things.

Chapter 5: Explanation of Arduino Components

An Arduino can very easily be built using a solderless bread board and just a few minutes of your time (once you are familiar with the process). Once you have built the board, the microcontroller can be programmed with the Arduino programming language. Then, you will be ready to use the board in your next do-it-yourself project.

What You Will Need

You only need a few inexpensive pieces to turn your solderless breadboard into an Arduino, including:

- **440 or 840 Tie Point Breadboard**
- **TTL-232R-3V3 USB to Serial Converter Cable**
- **Small Momentary Tact Switch**
- **16 MHz Clock Crystal**
- **1 Row Male Header Pins**
- **22 AWG Wire (selection of colors)**
- **1 Brown, Black, Red 10k Ohm Resistor**
- **2 Red, Red, Brown 220 Ohm Resistors**
- **2 22pF Capacitors**
- **2 10 uF Capacitors**

Step 1

Once you have gathered all of the necessary parts, you are ready to start building your Arduino breadboard. The first step is to set up power. For this particular model, a constant +5Volts of power will be provided. You will also set up a 7805 voltage regulator.

When looking at your breadboard, you will see squares with red and black + and – symbols on them. Begin by placing one 10uF capacitor here. Then you will need to add the 7805 voltage regulator to the breadboard. Be sure you are lining up the left leg of the 7805 with the power in, and the middle power up with the ground. Now you will need the second 10uF capacitor. Place this on the power rail. Finally, if you choose, include an LED status indicator on your breadboard. This is a good idea for troubleshooting. Connect the right and left power rails with a 220 resistor.

Step 2

For the second step, you will be preparing your chip. Each pin should align with a specific slot on the board. This will ensure your Arduino functions the way that you need it to.

Number on the Board	Corresponding Pin
1	Reset
2	Digital Pin 0 (RX)

3	Digital Pin 1 (TX)
4	Digital Pin 2
5	Digital Pin 3
6	Digital Pin 4
7	VCC
8	GND
9	XTAL 1
10	XTAL 2
11	Digital Pin 5
12	Digital Pin 6
13	Digital Pin 7
14	Digital Pin 8
15	Digital Pin 9 (PWM)
16	Digital Pin 10 (PWM)
17	Digital Pin 11 (PWM)
18	Digital Pin 12
19	Digital Pin 13 (LED)
20	AVCC
21	AREF
22	GND
23	Analog Input 0
24	Analog Input 1

25	Analog Input 2
26	Analog Input 3
27	Analog Input 4
28	Analog Input 5

Step 3

Once your pins are in place, add the tact switch near pin 1. This will reset your Arduino breadboard when necessary. Then, connect a small jumper wire between the bottom leg of the switch and pin 1. The next step is to connect the 10K resistor between pin row 1 and the power switch. The final thing you will need to do in this area is connect a GND wire to the top leg.

Next, connect power and GND jumpers between VCC (pin 7) and GND (pin 8). The 16 MHz clock crystal should then be added to pins 9 and 1-. Next, add the .22pF capacitors from these pins to GND. You can stop here if you choose, and add a programming chip. If you are interested in setting the breadboard up for programming, however, continue reading.

Step 4

The connections you will need for programming include the pins GND, NC, 5V, TX, RX, and NC. Connect the GND wire from the power rail to the GND pin. Add a power wire to the 5V pin. Finally, connect a wire between the TX pin and the RX pin. Your Arduino breadboard is now ready to be programmed. You can do this by using the USB – Serial Converter Cable from the list of necessary items.

How to Build a Swimming Electronic Snake

When built correctly, this snake is waterproof and can be controlled using a remote controller. If this is your first attempt at an Arduino project, you may want to choose a simpler option from one of the later chapters to start with. While this section will be fun to read, you may want to attempt building the light-up, rain-sensing umbrella from Chapter 8, the biking jacket with blinking turn signals from Chapter 9, or the Arduino gas sensor from Chapter 10 first.

Electronic Items

You will need:

- Arduino Uno
- Seeeduino Mega
- 10 Servo Motors (Remember that you get what you pay for. The nylon gears in these

motors may wear out quickly if you choose lower quality motors.)

- Servo Extension Wire
- Servo Motor Shield
- 2 Xbee Series 1
- Xbee Explorer
- Xbee Breakout (with 2 rows Xbee 2mm female headers and 2 rows of 10 male header pins)
- 3 6V NiMh Battery packs

Mechanical Hardware

- Urethane Sealant
- Marine Epoxy Sealant
- Marine Grease
- Nylon String
- Green Loctite
- 2" x 10" of 1/8" Thick Rubber
- 3 Strips Each of Carbon Fiber – 1/32", 1" x 12"
- 2 2.5 to 1.25" Shop Vac Vacuum Reducer
- O Rings
- 5/16" Hose Clamp
- Convoluted Hose Clamp
- 5/16" Tubing

- 5 Servo Brackets
- 5 Injection Molded Servo Hinge
- 5' x 2.5" Urethane Dust Collection Tube
- 5 Lynxmotion C-Brackets
- 5 Lynxmotion Servo Brackets

Tools

- Solder Iron + Solder
- Drill
- 3mm Drill Bit
- Small Screwdriver
- Needlenose Pliers
- Wire Strippers
- Wires
- Angle Snips
- Hack saw
- 2-56 nuts, bolts, and screws, either lock or toothed
- 4-40 nuts, bolts, and screws, either lock or toothed

Step 1

Once you have gathered all of the various tools, electronic items, and hardware, it is time to begin your project. You will start by waterproofing the 10 Servo motors. Begin by applying the silicon marine sealant around the plastic seams of the motor. You should also apply it to the bottom of the motor (where the screws are located) and around the wire insertion area. You should let this dry for a minimum of 24 hours.

Next, unscrew the round plastic that makes up the top of the motor. Slip an O-ring around the shaft after using a thin layer of marine grease on it. Then, replace the plastic top. This is also known as the servo horn.

Step 2

For this step, you will be preparing the carbon fiber for use. Cut the 12" x 1" strips into 3 separate pieces. This will result in 4" strips. If you have a dremel handy, you can round the corners so they are not jagged from cutting. Then, place the servo brackets 3 inches apart on the strips. Make markings where the bracket holes line up. Take a 3mm drill bit and drill into the carbon fiber, making holes where the markings are. You will need to do this with 7 of your 4" strips of carbon fiber.

Step 3

In this step, you will be building the frame of your robotic snake. Begin by using the screws that come with the brackets to attach the carbon fiber. Be sure you use the bolt that came with the bracket as well. Then, take the rubber and line it up with the middle section of the c-bracket. Use these as your guideline to cut 5 pieces of rubber that are approximately 1" x 2." Draw a dot where the holes of the bracket align with the rubber. Then, poke a hole through the rubber so you can more easily insert the 2-56 screws. These should go through the black clamp, through the rubber, and through the red bracket.

Step 4

In this step, you will be mounting the Servos motors. Your Servos should come with several parts. Begin with the rectangular cube and insert it into the four holes of the motor. The flat side should face outward. Adhere the injection molded joint on five of the motors and place them in the bracket. Use the 4x40 screws and a lock nut to screw the servo into the black servo bracket.

Step 5

In this step, you will be mounting the servos bracket to the c-bracket pairs. For the red brackets, the c-bracket should be put into place underneath of the servo bracket, but above the servo horn. A screw and bearing should be used to secure it. For the black brackets, the c-bracket should be slipped over the motor. This will cover most of its body. Once you secure these, you should have s snake-like structure that makes up the body of your robotic snake.

Step 6

To complete the body of your snake, line up the servo horns with the holes of the bracket. Ensure your horn is centered before screwing them together. If the brackets and motors do not rotate freely after being secured, apply grease between the brackets. For additional security, apply Loctite to the screws once you are sure they are in the correct position.

Step 7

In this step, you will be making the circuit board for your snake. Begin by soldering the male and female headers onto the Xbee Breakout board. Insert the Xbee. Then, take the Servo motor shield and solder it into the screw terminals. Once it has been soldered together, take your wires and connect the Xbee to the Arduino. Connect the 3.3Vin pin on the Xbee to the Arduino 3.3V pin. Jump the TX pin on the Xbee to the Arduino RX pin. Connect the Xbee ground to the Arduino ground pin. Finally, jump the power cord between the Arduino VIN pin and the 6V battery input.

Next, solder the wires from digital output pins for the number of servo motors you are using. You should take the dOUT wires from your Arduino, and then plug them into the servo cables. Screw the wires into the screw terminals. This will attach the 6V and ground from the batteries.

Step 8

Next you will need the code to make your snake swim. You can find this in the software library on the Servo Arduino library. You will need a code to generate wave locomotion using oscillation. This will create a sine wave that travels down the servos motors.

Step 9

In this step, you will create a free standing joystick controller for the snake. Begin by plugging the Xbee into the Xbee shield. Set them atop the Arduino and make 6 button inputs. These buttons should be connected to digital pins 2-7 on the Arduino. You will now upload a code from the Arduino library to take the button inputs and output them as movement in the snake.

Step 10

This is the step where you will add all of the wires to the snake. Use the wire extenders from the servo motors and extend the wires down the body of the snake. They should end just a few inches after the last bracket. If you want to, you can tape the wires to the carbon fiber so it is easier to put the carbon fiber on.

Step 11

In this step, you will attach the batteries using the 6V/GND wires so that your snake can operate. Attach one battery to each segment of carbon fiber, using two zip ties. You should also take the wire extensions from the Servo motor so that he battery power reaches the ground and Arduino at the front of the snake.

Step 12

This is the step where you add the on/off buttons. You may want to use one for the Arduino/Servos connection and one for the water pump. Be sure you turn on the snake before the pump, because running the water pump without water will cause it to dry out and burn up. Then, cut two pieces of rubber 1.75" in diameter. This should fit inside of the vacuum reducer. You should also cut two 2' long pieces of cord to help position the snake's body inside the vacuum reducer. You will need to cut a small slit for the wires in the rubber before placing it in the vacuum reducer. You will also attach the string here. You will have power and ground wires from the water pump, power and ground wires from the on/off switches, and one string running thorough both the rubber pad and the vacuum reducer. At the tail, you will only need the string on the outside to tether the snake. Next, take the 6V wire on the screw terminal and solder the on/off button to it.

Step 13

In this step, you will elongate the snake body and prepare the battery so the water pump can operate properly. Attach carbon fiber pieces that are 4" long at the head and tail ends of the snake. Solder a battery junction and the water pump together. Next, locate the wire that extends between the battery and pump. This is where you will need to solder the switch to turn your snake on and off. Use the zip ties to attach the battery to the carbon fiber next to the Arduino.

Step 14

In this step, you will be sealing the body of the snake and putting on the skin. Use caulk on either end of the vacuum reducer to cover the wires completely. Wait at least 24 hours for the caulk to dry before finishing the project. You can use hot glue to secure the wires and silica packs to absorb moisture if you choose. You should also take this opportunity to ensure the joints are moving freely. Add additional grease if necessary. Now, slip the skin over the body of the snake. Cut the tube length if necessary so that the carbon fiber fits into the end of the tube when positioned with the string. Tie the string in a knot once you have finished to prevent slippage. Finally, you need to put caps on the head and tail end of the snake using marine grease to keep water out.

Step 15

Now that the snake is fully assembled, you are ready to mount the water pump. Once mounted, the water pump should be located close to the head of the snake, but on the bottom side. It will be submerged during operation. Cut 5/16" plastic tubing to slip over the output nozzle of the pump. Then secure a hose-clamp at the joint of the tube. Use this plastic tubing to mount the pump. You can use a zip tie to secure it. If you are interested, you can even mount a GoPro on the snake.

Step 16

Now you are ready to test out your robotic water snake! Be sure to apply grease around the plastic buttons before taking it outside. Turn the snake on and place it in the water. Once you have placed the robotic snake in the water, you will be able to turn the pump on without drying it up. Use your remote controller to direct the motion of the snake.

Chapter 6: Getting started with Arduino

The first step in setting up your Arduino microcontroller will be to choose an Arduino board with which you want to work.

Choosing a Board

When looking at the options for Arduino Boards, there are a few factors you will want to consider before making a choice. Before deciding on a board, ask yourself the following questions:

How much power do I need to run the application I have in mind?

You might not know the exact measure of flash memory and processing power that you require for your project, but there is a clear difference between the functioning of a simple nightlight that changes colors and a robotic hand with many moving parts. The latter would require a more robust Arduino microcontroller board, with faster processing,more flash memory, and more SRAM than the more straightforward night light idea.

How many digital and analog pins will I require to have the functionality that I desire?

Again, you don't need to have an extremely specific idea in mind but knowing whether you need more pins or less will have a great effect on which board you choose. If you are going for a simple first project, you could get away with having less digital, PWM, and analog pins, while if you are looking to do something more complex, you will want to consider the boards with a great number of pins in general. Do I want this to be a wearable device?

There are a few options for wearable devices so, of course, this question will not entirely make the decision for you. It will, however, help narrow down the choices and steer you in a direction, with Lilypads and the Gemma or other comparable technologies being your best options. Do I want to connect to the Internet of Things? If so, how?

If you want connectivity to the Internet of Things, your work will be made much easier by the YÚN, the Tian, the Ethernet, the Leonardo ETH, or the Industrial 101. These have the capabilities of Ethernet connection as well as Wi-Fi capability so you will be able to connect to a network like the Internet and share data or interact with and control other devices on the Internet of Things. Getting Started on Arduino IDE The Arduino Software runs in an environment called IDE. This means that you will either need to download the desktop IDE to code in or code online on the online IDE. The first way that you might access IDE, downloading the desktop application, has a few options to suit the various devices that you might be using. First, there is the Windows desktop application. You can also access it from a Windows tablet or Windows phone with the Windows application. Next, there is the Macintosh OSX version, which allows IDE to run on Apple laptops and desktops, but not on Apple mobile devices like iPhones and iPads. Finally, there are three options for running Arduino IDE on Linux: the 32-bit, the 64-bit, and the Linux ARM version. If you prefer this option to the web browser option, you will simply need to visit the Arduino IDE site by heading to https:// www.arduino.cc/ en/ Main/ Software There, you can download the appropriate version of desktop IDE. Next, you will run the installation application, click through the options presented, and you should have a running Arduino IDE environment in just a few minutes.

This allows you to access the IDE software from Android devices and Apple mobile devices as well since it is based in a web browser that runs on its own platform rather than on the Android or iOS platforms. You can also run the web browser on various computer types, including Linux, Microsoft Windows, and Apple Macintosh. This will allow you to upload your sketches to the Cloud, that is, to store the information you have coded in a secure location that you can then re-access from another device by connection to the Internet. Coding a Program for Your Arduino Next you will write code for a program that you want the Arduino board to run. This allows you to see the entire code at once, allowing for easier debugging, or removing of errors.

Once you write the code, you will want to run it and troubleshoot or debug any errors that you find. You will best be able to do this by applying the coded program to the Arduino board and seeing if it runs. To do this, you will need to proceed to the next step of uploading your sketch. Connecting to the Arduino Board

Some of the boards come with built-in USB, mini-USB, or micro-USB ports. Examples would be the Uno and the Leonardo, for the more beginning stages of your Arduino career. Simply insert the appropriate end of the USB cord into your computer and the other end into the particular USB port that is present on the board you possess, and the Arduino IDE software should recognize the type of board it is. If it does not, you can always choose the correct board from a dropdown menu.

Sometimes you will need to use a TKDI cable or a breakout board in order to make the Arduino compatible with your computer. This means you will insert the TKDI into the TKDI port on the Arduino microcontroller board and then connect it either to your computer or to another board. If you connect the TKDI cable to a breakout board, you will do as you did with the USB-compatible boards: insert the appropriate end of the cord to the breakout board and the other end to the computer. Again, the computer's Arduino IDE software program should recognize your Arduino board, but you can always choose from a dropdown menu should it fail to recognize it. Uploading to the Arduino Board

To upload your sketch, the program you just created in code, you will need to select the correct board and port to which you would like to upload. It should be easy enough to select the correct board, as you simply look for the board title that matches the name of the type of board you are using.

To select the correct serial port, the options you might choose are as follows:

Mac

Use /dev/ tty.usbmodem241 for the Uno, Mega2560 or Leonardo.

Use /dev/ tty.usbserial-1B1 for Duemilanove or earlier Arduino boards.

Use /dev/ tty.USA19QW1b1P1.1 for anything else connected by a USB-to-serial adapter.

Windows

Use COM1 or COM2 for a serial board.

Use COM4, COM5, or COM7 or higher for a USB-connected board.

Look in Windows Device Manager to determine which port the device you are using is utilizing.

Linux

Use /dev/ ttyACMx for a serial

port.

Use /dev/ ttyUSBx or something like it for a USB port. Once you have selected the correct board and port, click Upload and choose which Sketch to upload from the menu that appears. If you have a newer Arduino board, you will be able to upload the new sketch simply, but with the older boards, you must reset the board before uploading a new sketch, else you will have two, possibly conflicting sketches present in the board's memory, causing it to crash. Running the Arduino with Your Program

There are a few ways to power your Arduino once you have uploaded the program that you have coded to it. First, you can power it by the USB connection to another powered device, such as your computer. Second, you can power by Ethernet on boards with that capability. This means that by connecting to the network, you will be connected to a power source through the Ethernet. Finally, you can power most Arduino's by lithium polymer battery. Once power is connected, and the specified input is put into the microcontroller, it will perform the function for which it is intended.

Installing the Arduino IDE

Now that you know the different parts of the Arduino board, we can learn how to prepare the Arduino IDE. After learning this, we will be ready to upload out the first program to the board. You will learn how to setup the board and set it ready to receive the program through a USB cable.

Ensure that you have the Arduino board and a USB cable. After assembling these, the next step is to download the Arduino IDE. You can download this from the following URL:

https://www.arduino.cc/en/Main/Software

Download the right version of Arduino based on the operating system that you are using. Once the download completes, unzip the downloaded file.

You can now power your board. The board can draw power from a USB connection to your computer or from an external power supply. Just connect your Arduino board to your computer via a USB cable. You should see the green power LED glow.

It is now time to launch the Arduino IDE. Open the folder where you unzipped the Arduino IDE. Double the .exe file to start the IDE.

The software will be opened and you will be able to create a new project or open an existing one. To create a new project, click File then chooses New. To open an existing project, click File, choose Example, Basics and then Blink.

You need to select the type of board that you are using. To avoid any errors when you are loading programs from the IDE to the board, ensure that you select the correct board, that is, the type of board you select in the IDE must match the type of board that is connected to your computer via the USB cable.

To select the board, click Tools then choose Board.

Next, you should select the serial port of your Arduino board. Click Tools then choose Serial Port. If you find it hard to know the serial port, just disconnect the Arduino board from the computer then look for the entry that disappears. This should be the Arduino board. You can then reconnect the board and choose that port.

Anytime you need to load a program to the Arduino board, just click the Upload button on the IDE. Note that an Arduino program is referred to as a **sketch.**

Digital Input/Output

Digital signals are discrete values that either exists as 1 or 0. This is to mean 1 (High) implies presence of a signal while 0 (Low) represents the absence of a signal. Digital signal is therefore transmitted as binary codes represented by either presence or absence of current, 5v or ground, or presence or absence of a pulse.

Human beings are used to analog signals while robots, computers and most electronic circuits perceive digital signals. As stated earlier, a digital signal only has two states, that is, ON and OFF just like a two-way light switch on your wall.

Digital signals are used everywhere in Arduino programming except for the analog input that is meant specifically to tolerate analog signals. The ON or HIGH state of the digital signal will always equal the board voltage as either 3.3 volts or 5.0 volts. On the other hand, the LOW or OFF state is always represented by 0 volts.

In order to receive or send digital signals on the Arduino board, use only pins labeled 0-13. Again as explained earlier it is possible to set up the analog pins to act as digital pins. This is achievable through the use of the command: pinMode (pin label, value). The pin number here stands for an analog pin ranging from A0-A5, the value in the function is always either input or output.

You can use the same command to set up digital pins. First of all reference the digital pin for pinNumber instead of analog. It is also important to note that digital pins by default used as input pins so it is only required of you to set them to OUTPUT mode. To achieve this, use the command: digitalRead (pin label) where the digital component will be connected to the pin label. digitalRead (pin number) returns either HIGH or LOW as results.

When you want to send a digital signal to a digital pin from the IDE platform, you are supposed to use the code: digitalWrite(pin label, value) where pin label stands for the pin number from which the signal is coming from and the value can either be HIGH or LOW.

Arduino also uses the technique of Pulse Width Modulation to send Digital signal that is in the form of analog. The pin numbers responsible for this are: 3, 5, 6, 9, 10 and 11. And the command used here looks like this: analogWrite(pin label, value). The pin numbers are already provided up there and the value is an integer ranging from 0 (0%) and 100% (255).

Examples of digital signals

ON/OFF, Men's table/Women's table, pregnancy, death, consciousness and the list continues.

Sensors and interfaces used here may include: Relays, Circuit breakers, Switches, Buttons and many others.

Chapter 7: Basic digital Arduino programs

LED Blink

This is the most basic program in Arduino programming just like printing the word "hello world" in any other programming language. Since in Arduino programming there is no screen to print "hello world", we therefore blink an LED as our first test program. This is indeed a very simple program that is meant to give you a strong foundation as you invest into the world of circuit building through prototyping.

The Required Components

- One breadboard

- An Arduino Uno

- One LED

- Resistor (330 ohms)

- Two jumper wires

Circuit

The circuit is quite simple due to the small number of components, therefore just follow the simple circuit diagram below:

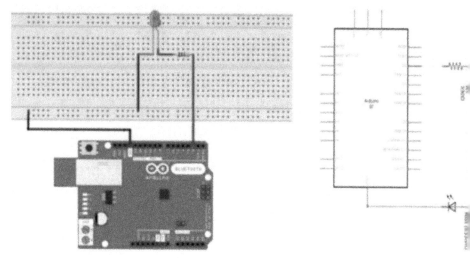

Finding the polarity of the LED

An LED has polarity, that is, negative and positive terminals. To determine this, hold the LED with the flat side facing you. The shorter leg on your left side is the negative terminal while the longer leg on your right is the positive terminal.

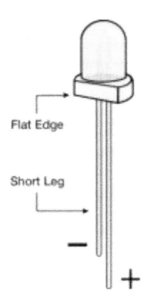

Flat Edge

Short Leg

—

+

Sketch

Quickly open the Arduino IDE on your computer, then a new sketch file on the New tab then begin writing your codes as shown below:

```
*/ Blink an LED, the codes below are meant to turn a
Light Emitting Diode connected to a digital pin
periodically. Pin number 13 is used since it has a
resistor in its circuit to limit current through the LED */

int ledPin = 13; // LED has been connected to digital pin
number                                                    13
void                                                 setup()
```

```
{
   ledPin(pinMode, OUTPUT); // the digital pin is set as
the                                                    output
   }
void                                                   loop()
   {
   digitalWrite(pinMode, HIGH); // the code is used to set
LED                                                       ON
      delay(1000);   //   delay   time   is   a   second
   digitalWrite(ledPin, LOW); // the code is used to set
LED                                                      OFF
      delay(1000);   //   delay   time   is   a   second
}
```

LED Blink without Delay

Sometimes you may wish to let the LED light without stopping and this calls for the use of another function other than delay ( ). The function for LED blinking without delay keep track of the time when the LED was turned ON and OFF. The using a loop ( ), it checks if sufficient time interval has passed so as to turn the LED ON if it was OFF and vice versa. The other components are the same as for the example above.

Here are the codes:

int ledPin = 13; // an LED has been connected to a digital pin number 13

int num = LOW; // int num has been declared and assigned LOW representing LED //previous value

```
long previousMillis = 0; // stores the value for when the
LED was last updated

long delay = 1000; // delay time is set to one second
(milliseconds)

void setup()

{

    pinMode(ledPin, OUTPUT); // the digital pin is set to
be the OUTPUT

}

void loop()

{

// the codes are the ones to control the lighting of the
LED.

if (millis() - previousMillis > delay)

    {

    previousMillis = millis(); // recalls the previous time
the LED blinked

// the codes below turns the LED ON in case it was OFF
and vice-versa.

if (num == LOW)

    num = HIGH;
```

```
else

  num = LOW;

  digitalWrite(ledPin, num);

 }

}
```

Fading an LED

For this case we will be using the analogWrite ( ) function to initiate the fading process an LED connected to the Arduino board. This is possible because analogWrite ( ) function uses Pulse Width Modulation technique which is able to turn on and off a digital pin quickly in different ratios thereby creating the fading effect. The components are still the same with the first example including the circuit. The only difference is noticed in the codes as shown below:

```
/*
Fade
```

Fade

```
This example illustrates the use of the function
analogWrite ( ) to control the fading of an LED*/

int ledPin = 6;     // LED is attached to the PMW pin
number 6

int brightness = 0; // current brightness of the LED
```

```
int fadeStep = 6; // the number of steps to fade the
LED through


void loop()
  {
      //code used to set the brightness of the LED on pin
6:
   analogWrite(ledPin, brightness);
      //code meant to change LED brightness for the next
step through the
      //loop:
   brightness = brightness + fadeStep;
     //codes used to reverse the fading direction at the
ends of each previous
   //fade:
   if (brightness == 0 || brightness == 255)
     {
        fadeStep = -fadeStep ;
     }
     // our delat time is 30 milliseconds so as to realize the
dimming effect
```

```
delay(300);

}
```

Arduino Button

This is typically a button that connects two points in a circuit. When pressed, the button completes the circuit between these two points as in lighting an LED.

Components

- A pushbutton
- One Arduino Uno
- One Light Emitting Diode
- Three connecting wires.
- 2.2 kilo ohms

Procedure

Your circuit should look like the one below:

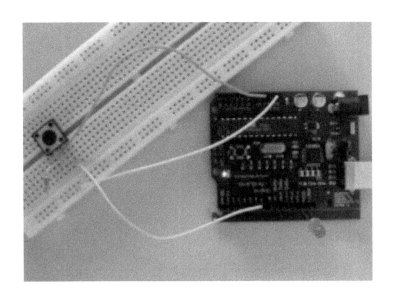

The codes for this project are written below:

int outPin = 14; // the LED has been connected to pin number 14

int inPin = 3; // our input pin for a pushbutton will be pin number 3

int num = 0; // variable declaration; used to read the pin status

void setup() {

  pinMode(outPin, OUTPUT); // LED will be used as the OUTPUT

  pinMode(inPin, INPUT); // pushbutton shall be our INPUT for this case

}

```
void loop()

    {

        num = digitalRead(inPin); // the code is used to
read value of the input

    if (num == HIGH) { // checks whether the button is
released (HIGH input)

    digitalWrite(outPin, LOW); // turns OFF the LED

    }

else

    {

    digitalWrite(outPin, HIGH); // turns the LED ON

    }

}
```

Arduino Pushbutton as a Debounce

This example is similar to the above exercise apart from the function of the pushbutton. The pushbutton debounces the input that is to mean without pressing the button represents a code similar to multiple presses.

The components and the circuit board is the same as the above example. So we will go direct to the codes as that we highlight the difference.

Code

```
int inPin = 6;      // the input has been assigned to pin number 6

int outPin = 11;   // the output has been assigned to pin number 11


int position = HIGH; // shows the current state of the output pin number 11

int display; //indicates the current reading of the input pin number 6

int previous = LOW; // the previous reading the input pin assigned LOW


long time = 0; // the variable time represents the period when the output was //toggled

long debounce =100; // the debounce time has been assigned

void setup()

{

    pinMode(inPin, INPUT);

    pinMode(outPin, OUTPUT);

}

void loop()
```

```
{
  display = digitalRead(inPin);

  if (display == HIGH && previous == LOW && millis() -
  time > debounce) {

    // ... the function returns an inverted output

    if (position == HIGH)

      position = LOW;

    else

      position = HIGH;

                // ... function recalls the time when
          button was pressed
                time = millis();
  }

                digitalWrite(outPin, position);
                previous = display;
}
```

Creating a Loop

Components required

- Six Light Emitting Diodes
- Six 220 Ohm resistors

- Seven jumper wires

- One Arduino Uno

In this example we shall six LEDs to demonstrate sequential blinking using the function digitalWrite(pin label, LOW/HIGH) together with delay ( ).

Circuit

Code

int timer = 120; // timing reduces with an increase in the time number.

int pins[] = { 2,3, 4, 5, 6, 7, 8 }; // pin numbers as an array of

int value_pins = 6; // array length represented by the number of pins

void setup()

```
{
    int j;

for (j = 0; j< value pins; j++) // the array elements as numbered from 0 //to value_pins - 1

pinMode(pins[j], OUTPUT); // each pin has been set as an output

}

void loop()

{

int j;

for (j = 0; j < num_pins; j++)

    {

// a loop is set through each output pin...

digitalWrite(pins[j], HIGH); // function to turn the output pin   ON,

delay(timer);              // delay function,

digitalWrite(pins[j], LOW); // function to turn the output pin OFF

        }

for (j = value_pins - 1; j >= 0; j--)
```

```
      {
digitalWrite(pins[j], HIGH);
delay(timer);
digitalWrite(pins[j], LOW);
          }
}
```

Chapter 8:Basic analog Arduino programs

Analog Input

In this project we shall use a potentiometer as the source of analog input signal to the Arduino board. Ideally, the potentiometer is able to vary resistance (variable resistance) which can then be read by the Arduino board as analog input. We are going to use the already fixed LED pin 11 on the Arduino board as part of our project.

Components required

☐   A potentiometer

☐   An Arduino project for LED lighting

☐   Three jumper wires

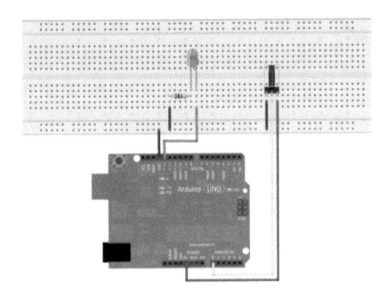

<u>Sketch</u>

/* potentiometer project under AnalogInput

This project aims to turn ON and OFF a light Emitting Diode periodically. The amount of light of the LED depends on the value of resistance of the potentiometer used. Increasing resistance reduces the amount of light and vice versa.

*/

int num = 0; //this variable stores the input value from the sensor output, //initially assigned 0

void setup()

{

```
pinMode(ledPin, OUTPUT); // function declares the LED
as an OUTPUT

}

void loop()

{

num = analogRead(inPin);     // function to read the
value of sensor //output

digitalWrite(ledPin, HIGH);  // function to turn the LED
ON

delay(num);              // delay function to stop the
program for a while

digitalWrite(ledPin, LOW);   // function to turn OFF the
LED

delay(num);                  // function stops the program
for a while

}
```

Knock Sensor

For this kind of a project, we shall employ the use of a piezo element and trap its sound as the analog input into the Arduino board. The processor of the board is able to read analog signals with the aid of its ADC (analog to digital Converter). The Piezo element (knock sensor) is just but an electronic device that is capable of playing tones and detect tones at the same. The Arduino board detects the sound levels as voltage levels, transform the voltage level to a corresponding value ranging from 0 to 1024 for voltages of 0 to 5.0 volts.

Remember that the Piezo element has polarity, black wire representing the negative terminal while the red wire represents the positive terminal.

In the sketch, we will try to capture the sound level (knock) of the Piezo element and confirm that it is above a certain threshold then send a "Knock" string a signal to the Arduino IDE platform.

Circuit

Sketch

```
/* Knock Sensor
```

In this project we are using the Piezo element as a knock sensor. We therefore have to listen to the sound level, if the signal goes beyond a specified threshold.

```
void setup()

{

    pinMode(ledPin, OUTPUT); // function declares the
ledPin as the OUTPUT

    Serial.begin(9600); // indicate the use of serial port

}

void loop()

{

    num = analogRead(knockSensor); // function is used
to read the value of the  //sensor and store it in the
variable num

if (num >= THRESHOLD)

    {

statePin = !statePin; // function that is used to toggle
the status of the ledPin though it does not use time
cycle

digitalWrite(ledPin, statePin); // function to turn LED ON
or OFF
```

```
Serial.println("Knock!"); // function sends the string
"Knock!" through //the serial port to the computer then
a newline

delay(100); // a very short delay in order to prevent
serial port from //overloading

  }

}
```

Arduino Smoothing

Involves the use of arrays where the sketch is supposed
to read analog input repeatedly, calculate the running
average and finally print the result.

<u>Sketch</u>

```
int readings[VALUES];        // array declaration to
represent readings from the //analog input

int index = 0;   // variable declaration and initialization

int total = 0;  // variable declaration and initialization

int average = 0; // variable declaration and initialization

int inputPin = 0; // variable declaration and initialization
```

```
void setup()

{

 Serial.begin(9600); // function used to create a serial
communication with the //computer

for (int j = 0; j < VALUES; j++)

readings[j] = 0; //setting all the initial readings to 0

}

void loop()
```

Printing Analog Input (Graphing)

This project demonstrate the how to read analog data, convert the signal into voltage levels and finally print t.

Components Required

☐   One breadboard

☐   One Arduino Uno

☐   One Potentiometer 5 kilo ohms

☐   Two jumper wires

☐   Eight LEDs

Circuit

The circuit diagram and the components on the diagram are shown below:

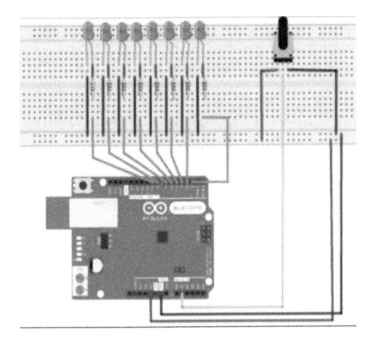

Sketch

*/

// the constants used below are to remain the same all through:

const int analogPin = A0; // the potentiometer has been attached to this pin

const int ledCount = 8; // representing the number of pins that will produce //the graphing effect

```
int ledPins[] = {3, 4, 5, 6, 7, 8, 9, 10}; // pin numbers
where the LEDs will //be attached forming an array of
pins

void setup()

{

    // a loop over the pin array thereby setting them as
the OUPUT:

for (int firstLed = 0; firstLed < ledCount; firstLed++)

    {

        pinMode(ledPins[firstLed], OUTPUT);

    }

}

void loop()

{

// the code below reads the potentiometer output to
use as the system input:

int sensorOutput = analogRead(analogPin);

// copy the result to a range of LEDs from 0 to 7:

int ledLevel = map(sensoroutput, 0, 1023, 0,
ledCount);

// a loop over the pin array:
```

```
for (int firstLed = 0; firstLed < ledCount; firstLed++)

{

// when the array element has an index which is less
than ledLevel then

// turn ON the pin for this particular element:

if (firstLed < ledLevel)

        {

    digitalWrite(ledPins[firstLed], HIGH);

        }

// function to turn OFF all other pins whose array
element have indices higher     //than the ledLevel:

    else

        {

        digitalWrite(ledPins[firstLed], LOW);

        }

    }

}
```

It is equally important to NOTE the results of this project: The eight LEDs will turn ON one after another with an increase in the value of the analog reading and they will be again turning OFF one by one on decreasing the value of analog reading.

Chapter 9: Arduino programming tools

Arduino Control Statements

Control structures involved in decision making demand that the person doing the actual programming (programmer) clarifies and specifies certain conditions that will be tested and evaluated by the program itself. These condition should be written along with some statements that will be executed if the condition is to return a value. Otherwise, other statements will be executed so as to return a false response or outcome for the condition.

Most of the programming languages have a general

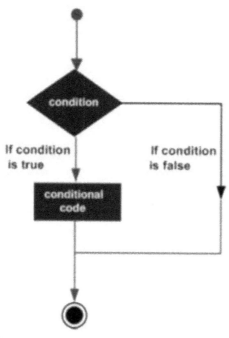

format for decision making structures as illustrated below:

The statements within the control structure (condition) as mean to coordinate the flow of program execution and are therefore referred to as Source Code Control Statements.

These are statements include:

If statement

If....else statement

If...else if...else statement

Switch case statement

Conditional operator?

Again just to emphasize, these statements are very important in navigating through various loops and sections in a program. Executing one part at a time and using the results to instruct the processor on the next block of codes to be executed.

If statement

This particular structure uses expressions in parenthesis together with statements or block of statements in the next line of codes. When the expression is true, then the processor is instructed to execute the block of statements or statements that were included in this condition. And if the expression is false, the processor skips the block of statements or statements and gets to the next line of codes. If statement takes two kinds of forms as explained below:

First form
```
{
if                                             (expression)
block of statements;
}
```

Second form

```
if                                             (expression)

{
statements;
}
```

Execution Sequence of If Statement

The order of execution for if statement is summarized

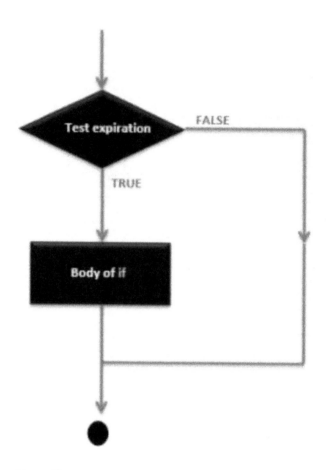

below by the diagram:

Example in a program:

```
/*      definition     of      Global     variables    */
int             X              =              5               ;
```

```
int              Y=              9              ;
Void                  setup                   ()
{

}
Void                  loop                    ()
{
/* this section is used to check the boolean
condition                                    */
    if (X > Y) /* when the condition is true then the
processor is to execute the
                statement                  below*/
                                             Y++;
/* this part is use to check the boolean condition
*/
    If ( ( X>Y ) && ( Y!=0 )) /* when this condition
is true then the processor executes the statement
below*/

    {

                                           X+=Y;
                                            Y--;
                                              }

}
```

The If...else statement

This structure provides an alternative statement to be executed in case the condition is false, that is to mean when if statement is false, then there is an optional way out since there is a provision of an optional else statement to be executed.

<u>Syntax</u>

```
if                                              (expression)
{
    statements;  //these statements are executed
only      when      the      condition      is      true
}
else
{
    statements;  // optional statements to be
executed   in   case   the   expression   is   false.
}
```

Summary of the execution sequence

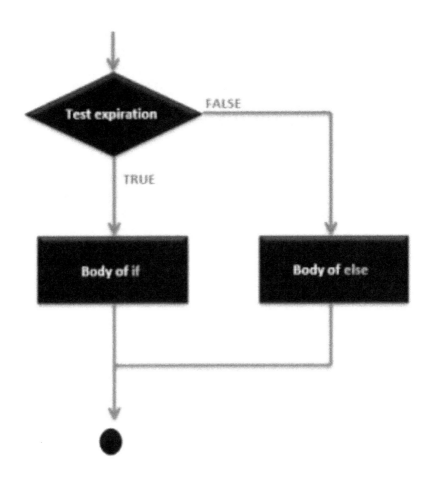

Example in a program

```
/*    definition    of    Global    variables    */
int          X          =          6          ;
int                Y=                8          ;
Void                  setup                    ()
{
}
Void                  loop                     ()
```

```
{
/* this section is used to check the boolean
condition                                        */
    if (X > Y) /* when the condition is true then the
processor is to execute the

                    statement                    below*/
    {

                                                    X++;

        }
    else

        {

        Y-=X

        }

    }
```

If...else if...else statement

This is a special control structure where an if statement is followed by an optional else..if...else control structure. Such an expression is quite important in navigating through conditions to test whether they are true or false.

NOTE: Always remember the following points while using If...else if...else statement:

It is possible for an **if statement** to have none or just one else statement, and the if statement must always come after any else if's.

It is lawful for an **if statement** to have none or many else if statements that must always come before the else statement.

All else if or else statements succeeded by an else if will never be executed since the processor goes by a mode of priority.

Syntax

```
if                    (first                    expression)
                                                         {
        statements   or   block   of   statements;
                                                         }
    else              if(second                expression)
                                                         {
        statements   or   block   of   statements;
    }
    .              //other else if statements

    .

    .

    .

    else
                                                         {
    statements      or      block    of    statements;
        }
```

Example in a program

```
/*    definition    of    Global    variables    */
int           X              =            5         ;
int           Y=                    9                ;
int                                           Z=15;
Void                        setup                  ()
{

}
Void                        loop                   ()
{
```

```
    /* checks if the boolean condition below is true
or                       false                    */
    if (X > Y) /* when the condition is true the
processor is instructed to execute the statements
below*/

    {

                                              X++;
                                               }
    /* checks if the boolean condition below is true
or                       false                    */
    else if ((X==Y )||( Y < Z) ) /* when the condition
is true the processor is instructed to execute the
statements                   below                 */
                                                {
                      Z=Y*                      X;
                                                }
    else

                                           Z++;

    }
```

Switch Case Statement

This kind of control structure works in a similar manner with if statements where the programmer is able to specify the different levels of codes that will be executed for different conditions.

A **switch** statement is instructed to compare the value of some variables against the specified values written within the **case** statement hence the name switch case. So the processor looks for a case statement with similar value to that of the switch statement then executes the codes in that particular case statement.

A **break** statement is used at the end of each case statement to enable the execution to exit at the end of each case. Without a break, execution will go through a state called **falling-through** where the switch statement will go on running the following until that point when there will a break or typically at the end of the switch statement.

Syntax

```
switch                                          (variable)
{
            name        of        the        case:
    //    statements    or    block    of    statements
                                                break;
                                                }
                    name                of        case:
                                                {
    //    statements    or    block    of    statements
                                                break;
                                                }
                        default                    case:
                                                {
    //    statements    or    block    of    statements
            break;

                                                }

    }
```

Example in a program:

We will use a very simple example where we will assume a variable with only three states, that is, high, low and mid representing logic levels of 0, 1 and 2. The program is supposed to switch the code according to the right routine. The codes would therefore look like this:

```
switch                    (variable              state)
{
    case 0: Low();
       break;
    case 1: Mid();
       break;
    case 2: High();
       break;

          default case:
          Display ("Invalid state!");
       }
```

Conditional Operator?

Conditional operator remains to be the only ternary operator in Arduino programming as well as in C programming language.

<u>Syntax</u>

First expression? second expression: third expression

Explanation: The first expression is executed first then depending on the outcome of this first execution, the subsequent expressions are either processed or skipped. That is to mean, when the outcome of expression is true, then the second one is executed and the sequence continues. When the first expression gives a false result then the execution skips expression two and processes expression three. Expression should give a result of either true or false depending on the condition to be satisfied.

Example in a program:

```
/*       Find       min(x,       y):       */
min   =   (   x   >   y   )   ?   x   :   y;
/* this portion is supposed to Convert a
small     letter     to     a     capital:     */
/* (parentheses may not necessarily be
required     in     this     case)     */
z = ( z >= 'x' && x <= 'c' ) ? ( z - 45 ) : z;
```

Some of the rules to take care of while working with condition operator:

☐ **Always ensure that the first expression is of a scalar type.**

☐ **For the subsequent expressions, keep in mind the following:**

- If they are two, then both must be of arithmetic type

- If they are two, then both should be evaluated by simple arithmetic conversions which eventually will determine the resulting type.

- If they are two, they should both use the void set up giving a result which is void in nature.

Arduino Programming Loops

Programming loops are more or less like control structures that provide for more complicated paths for execution.

Therefore a loop statement makes a provision for the execution to process statements or a block of statements in a multiple of times. The general

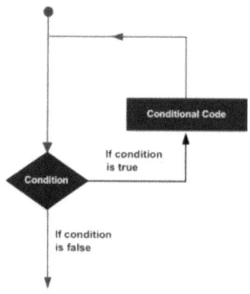

schematic diagram is shown below:

Arduino programming together with C language provides the following types of loops:

- While loop
- Do...while loop

- For loop
- Nested loop
- Infinite loop

While Loop

This loop continues to execute or process infinitely until that point in time when the expression inside the parenthesis gives a false result. Actually while loop will never exit unless something changes with the nested variables.

<u>Syntax</u>

while(expression)

{

statements   or   block   of   statements;
}

Do...while loop

Do...while loop is similar to while loop only that in while loop execution, the condition for loop-continuation is tested right at the commencement of loop before execution gets to the body of the loop. While in do...while loop, execution tests the body of the loop before checking the condition for loop-continuation.

After execution of a do...while loop execution (after termination), execution actually goes on to process those statements after the while statement.

<u>Syntax</u>

Do

```
{
    Statements    or    block    of    statements;
}
```

while (expression);

For loop

For this kind of a loop, the statements are executed for a predetermined number of successions. Within the for loop expression, the control expression is initialized, tested and changed during execution.

This presents a very easy to debug arrangement where the structure has a looping behavior which is entirely independent of the activities happening inside the loop.

For loop has three expressions inside the parenthesis which controls its operation. The expressions are separated by with semicolons.

<u>Syntax</u>

```
for ( expression initialization; control part; increment        or        decrement        portion)
{
    // statements or block of statements
}
```

Example in a program:

```
for(counter=3;counter              >=10;counter++)
{
    //statements or block of statements will be
```

executed   10   times
}

Nested Loop

This is a technique where you can use a loop inside another loop as illustrated below by the syntax.

<u>Syntax</u>

```
for (expression initialization ;control part;
increment or decrement portion)
{
    // statements or a block of statements
for (expression initialization ;control part;
increment or decrement portion)
{
    // statements or a block of statements
}
}
```

Example in a program:

```
for(counter=0;counter<=10;counter++)
{
    //statements or a block of statements will be
executed                    10                    times
                        for(j=0;j<=100;j++)
                        {
    //statements or a block of statements will
be          executed          101          times
                        }
}
```

Infinite Loop

As the name suggests, this is a loop without a point of termination therefore executes infinite number of times.

<u>Syntax</u>

1. When using for loop

```
for                                    (;;)
                                        {
    // statements or a block of statements
}
```

2. Using while loop

```
while(expression)
                                        {
        // statements or a block of statements
}
```

3. Using do...while loop

```
Do
                                        {
    Statements or a Block of statements;
}
while(expression);
```

Arduino Functions

These are statements per see that allow programmers to structure their programs in parts or segments that are meant to perform particular tasks at a time. For example, a function would be helpful when one wants to perform a particular task a multiple times in a program.

Advantages of code segmentation into standardized fragments:

☐   Segmented codes presents a more organized work enhancing easier conceptualization such codes.

☐   During modification, code fragments are least liable to error since any mistake is easily noticeable.

☐   Codes stay compact and there is reduced space since most of the codes are reused several times.

☐   Functions presents a modular set up of codes that is easy to read and can be reused in other sections.

Arduino programming provides for two compulsory functions, that is, set up ( ) and loop ( ). Other functions must be created right outside of the brackets of the above functions.

Common syntax defining a function:

Return type function name (first argument, second argument, ...)

{

       Statements or a block of statements

}

Explanation:

Return type: the type of value that is returned by the function, for example, any data type.

Function name: Identifier or title by which this function can be recalled.

First argument, second argument...: These are parameters that are used to define the data type.

Statements or a block of statements: Incorporates the statements or the body of the function itself.

Function Declaration

Any function is supposed to be declared outside other functions, that is, below or above loop ( ) function.

Function declaration can take two forms namely:

☐   Just writing the function prototype just above the loop ( ) function and this form consists of: Return type, name, and argument type. Function prototype is always followed by a semi-colon.

Example in a program:

```
int aver_func (int a, int b) // declaration of the
efunction
{
  int c=0;
    c= a+b ;
    return z; // return the result's value
}
void setup ()

{
    Statements // block of statements
}
Void loop ()
{
  int result =0 ;
    result = Aver_func (8,7) ; // part of the program
referred to as a function call
}
```

☐ The function declaration part or function definition is declared below the loop ( ) function and consists of: Return type, name and argument type.

Example in a program:

```
int aver_func (int , int ) ; // part of the program called a
function prototype
void setup ()
{
   Statements //   block of statements
}
Void loop ()
{
  int result =0 ;
      result = Aver_func (9,10) ; // part of the program
called a function call
}
int Aver_func (int a, int b) // declaration of this function
{
    int b=0;
    b= a+c ;
    return b; // return the resultant value of b
}
```

Arduino Programming- Strings

The two types of strings used in Arduino programming are:

Character arrays which are equivalent to strings in C programming language

Arduino String that enables programmers to use a string object as part the sketch.

So in this chapter we will be able to identify strings, objects and which types of strings to use in Arduino programming (sketches).

String of Character Arrays

This is typically a series of characters of the data type char also called an array consisting char variables. An array therefore would mean a collection texts of the same data type and stored in a memory.

However a string is a special type of array with an extra element always zero at the end of it.

Example in a program:

```
void setup()
{
   char go_str[7]; // an array which can accommodate
string made up of six characters
   Serial.begin(10000);
   go_str[0] = 'G'; // this string is made up of six
characters
   go_str[1] = 'o';
```

```
go_str[2] = 'o';
go_str[3] = 'd';
go_str[4] = 'i';

go_str[5] = 'e';
go_str[6] = 0; // the 7th array element called a null
terminator
Serial.println(go_str);
}
void loop()
{

}
```

This same example can be rewritten in a more convenient way as shown below:

```
void setup()
{
   char go_str[] = "Goddie";
   Serial.begin(10000);
   Serial.println(go_str);
}
void loop()
{

}
```

Before this string is executed, the compiler is supposed to calculate its size and automatically terminate it using the null terminator.

Manipulation of a String Array:

We will consider the sketch below to explain how to manipulate a string array.

```
void setup()
{
 char take[] = "I do not take mangoes and tea"; // creating a string array
    Serial.begin(10000);
        // the codes below are used to print the string
    Serial.println(take);
        // the codes below are used to delete part of the string
    take[13] = 0;
  Serial.println(take);
        // the codes below explain how to substitute a text into an existing string
    take[13] = ' '; // the null terminator replaced with a space
    take[18] = 'e'; // point to insert the next new word
    take[19] = 'g';
    take[20] = 'g';

    take[21] = 0; // null terminator used to terminate the string
    Serial.println(take);
}
void loop()
 {
 }
```

Result

☐   I do not take mangoes and tea

☐   I do not take mangoes

☐   I do not take mangoes and egg

Explanation

First you need to create and print a string. For the sketch above, a new string was created and displayed on the Serial Monitor window.

The second process is to shorten the string using a null terminator. That means when printing the new string, characters are displayed up to that point where there is the null terminator.

The next procedure is to change a word in a string. Firstly you have to replace the new null terminator with a space so that the string is restored to its original format. The next step is to replace the individual characters in the word to be replaced, that is, t-e-a with e-g-g.

Arrays and strings have specified bounds that restrict programmers to always work within those restrictions. In the above example, we created an array of 38 characters long and therefore trying to copy and array which is longer that this may be difficult. The copied longer array will be copied over the end of the created array.

Arduino Programming- Time

Arduino programming has a total of four time manipulation functions as listed below:

☐ Delay ( ) function

☐ Delaymicroseconds ( ) function

☐ Millis ( ) function

☐ Micros ( ) function

We will discuss each of these time functions and highlight their importance in Arduino programming.

Delay ( ) function

This presents the simplest time manipulation function among the four functions. Only a single integer is used as its input or argument. This integer represents a waiting time in milliseconds that instructs the program to wait until it moves on to the next group of codes where it will encounter the delay ( ) function.

Usually this function is not recommended to instruct your code to wait as it is associated with a phenomenon called "blocking".

DelayMicroseconds ( ) function

Just lie the delay ( ) function, delayMicroseconds ( ) also accepts only a single integer as its argument or input. The integer here represents time in microseconds which is equivalent to a thousandth of a millisecond or a millionth of a second in this case.

Record time that has been tested and proved to be able to produce an accurate delay is 16383 which is subject to change depending on future inventions in Arduino boards' production. However, for delays less than thousand microseconds, it is advisable to use the delay ( ) function.

Millis ( ) function

The time delay used here is milliseconds, which is to mean, immediately the Arduino board runs a program, it returns a number of milliseconds. This delay time at times goes back to zero a phenomenon called "overflowing" after around 50 or so days.

Syntax

millis () ; // this function returns milliseconds from when the program begins.

Example in a program:

```
unsigned double delay time;
void setup(){
    Serial.begin(9600);
```

```
}
  void loop()
{
 Serial.print("delay time:");
 delay time = millis();
      //the codes below will print time since the program
begun
 Serial.println(delay time);
      //this code dictate that you will have to wait for a
second to prevent sending //massive amounts of data
delay time(1000);
}
```

Micros ( ) function

This function also returns the amount of time from the beginning of the program, the time is expressed in microseconds. Overflowing phenomenon also happens here after a period of about 70 minutes.

<u>Syntax</u>

micros () ; // the function is supposed to return a time period in microseconds after the program ahs begun.

Example in a program

```
unsigned double delay time;
void setup(){
```

```
   Serial.begin(9600);
}
void loop(){
   Serial.print("delay Time:");
delay time = micros();
        //the codes below prints time period  since
program begun

   Serial.println(delay time);
        // this code dictate that you will have to wait for a
second to prevent //sending massive amounts of data
delay time(1000);


}
```

Arduino programming- Arrays

An array is a consecutive collection of elements of the same data type located in consecutive memory locations.

In locating a particular element in array, we must specify its name and the name of its storage location. Therefore an array has two important features, that is, name and location. Identifying an array is done by giving that particular element a name then by the element's position in a square bracket [ ]. The first element (called zero element) has a subscript zero and the subsequent elements can be represented by C[1], C[2], C[3] and the rest as shown in the figure below:

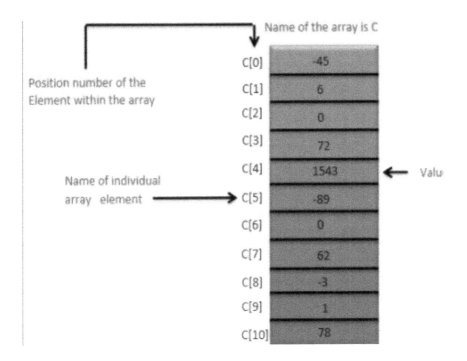

The above array is called C with 11 elements. Each element has a value for example C[10] has a value of 78.

We can therefore write programs to manipulate these values, for example, to print the sum of the values of the first three elements in the array we can write:

Serial.print (C[0] + C[1] + C[2]);

Again we can write another program to multiply the value of C[8] by 6 and assign the result to a variable called y:

x = C[8] * 6;

Arrays Declaration

Arrays declaration helps to specify the type of element and the total number of elements in that array as illustrated below:

type arrayName [arraySize] ;

This instructs the compiler to reserve enough memory for the array. That is why the array size must be an integer. For example:

int D[32]; // array name is D with an array size of 32 integers

Examples of programs using Arrays

Array declaration and then using a loop in the initialization of the array elements:

```
int b[ 12 ] ; // array name is b with 12 integers as array size
void setup ()

{ }
void loop ()
{
  for ( int j = 0; j < 10; ++j ) // array initialization with elements
  {
      b[ j ] = 0; // this codes sets element at location j to
```

```
be 0
    Serial.print (j) ;
    Serial.print ('\r') ;
}
    for ( int i = 0; j=i < 10; ++i ) // specifies the output
of each array element's //value
    {
      Serial.print (n[i]) ;
      Serial.print ('\r') ;
    }

}
```

Array declaration and initialization using an initializer list:

```
// b is an array made up of 12 integers
int b[ 10 ] = { 23, 20, 48, 12, 16, 28, 87, 79, 69, 37,
58,17 } ;
void setup ()

{

}
void loop ()
{
   for ( int j = 0; j < 10; ++j ) // the codes are used for
initialization of elements //in the array from n to 0
   {
     Serial.print (j) ;
```

```
  Serial.print ('\r') ;
}
  for ( int i = 0; i < 10; ++i ) //codes that specify the
output of each array //element's value
  {
  Serial.print (n[i]) ;
  Serial.print ('\r') ;
  }

}
```

Multidimensional Arrays

An array of two dimensions mostly represent a table of elements consisting of rows and columns.

Some of the outstanding features of a multidimensional array:

☐   Has two subscripts representing the columns and rows of a table.

☐   The first subscript represent the elements' rows and the second subscript represents the elements' columns.

☐   Multidimensional arrays have two and more dimensions.

An example by declaration is shown below:

int c[3][3] = { { 3, 8 }, { 3, 7 } };

or int c[3][3] = { { 3 }, { 3, 9 } };

Summing all the Array elements

Those elements in an array normally represent values that are as a result of a calculation or those yet to be used in a particular math work. For example a professor may decide to enter the marks of students in a table forming an array then using the total to calculate the average marks of the class. The example below explains how this can be achieved using array functions.

const int arraySize = 5; // array size indicated by a variable called const and data type used is int

```
int c[ arraySize ] = { 80, 60, 50, 100, 70,};
int total = 0;
  void setup ()
{

}
  void loop ()
{
// the code below is used to get the sum of the contents
of array c
for ( int j = 0; j < arraySize; ++j )
   total += c[ j ];
Serial.print (" sum Total of elements of array c : ") ;
Serial.print(total) ;
}
```

Chapter 10: Input, Outputs, and Sensor

One conductor is going to be used to receive data, another will be used to send information, one is going to synchronize, and the other will choose which device it will communicate with. For this to function, it will mean it is set up as the connections full duplex. This means the data can be simultaneously received and sent. The largest baud rate can be far greater than the communication system housing the i2c.

Panel SPI Pin
>The SPI is going to use four wires.

1. **SS: this will be the slave selection wire**

2. SCK: this will be the serial clock driven by the master

3. **MISO: the master input and the slave result. which is going to be powered by the mater**

4. MOSI: the mast output and slave input driven by the master.

Some of the functions that you are going to use will have to include the SPI. H

SPI set clock divider (divider): this will set up the SPI clock divider which means that it is going to be relative to the system clock. With the AVR base panels, the divider is going to be available with two, four, eight, sixteen, thirty-two, sixty-four, and one hundred and twenty-eight. Your default setting will be SPI CLOCK DIV 4 which is going to set up the SPI clock to a quarter of the frequencies of the system's clock.

1. **Divider: this is going to be (SPI CLOCK DIV 2, SPI CLOCK DIV 4, etc.)**

2. SPI transfer (Val): the SPI is going to be assigned based on the sending and receiving that will occur at the same time. The data that is obtained will be returned in a standard Val form.

3. **SPI begin transaction (SPI setting (speed maximum, data order, data mode)) the top speed is going to be clocked with data order (MSBFIRST or LSBFIRST)**

There are going to be four modes of operation that the SPI is going to follow

1. **Mode 0 (default): the clock is naturally going to be low, and the data that is obtained from the transition can be visualized when the data itself goes from the bottom end of the spectrum to higher levels. This will be what is known as the leading edge.**

2. Mode 1: this is going to be considered the trailing edge whenever the data is going from high to low

3. **Mode 2: this is also going to be the leading edge when your data goes from high to low.**

4. Mode 3: the data here also goes from the low end of the spectrum to the high. In this instance, it is known in the industry as the trailing edge.

5. **SPI attach interrupt (handler): the function is going to be summoned as the slave device gets its data from the master.**

At this point in time, you are going to connect two Uno panels together with one being the slave and the other being the master.

Pin ten will be SS

Pin eleven will be MOSI

Pin twelve will be MISO

Pin thirteen will be SCK

The ground is going to be common, and in the following image, you are going to see the connection that is going to occur between both panels.

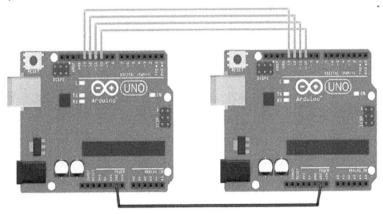

Advanced Strategies for Arduino

Speeding Up the Input and Output Access

On each AVR Arduino panel, the clock speed is going to be sixteen MHz. Every instruction that is located on the controller is going to be completed in under four cycles; therefore, you are going to be able to do four million instructions in a single second. But, the input-output speed is going to be a lot slower. This happens due to the digital write and digital read functions. Each time that a function is executed, there is going to be extra code that has to be executed as well. The additional code is going to end up being responsible for detecting and mapping out the digital pins to the output port. On every microcontroller, the input-output device will be allocated in a group of eight pins to a port which is going to be specially registered to the controller.

Therefore, the next question is going to be, how slow is it? You will figure this out by using this code.

You will be able to improve the program by wrapping the loop code into an infinite loop. This is going to speed up the execution since the CPU is going to be doing less of a function call. This should speed up your input and output so that it is up to ten percent faster. If you want to top the output speed, you are going to have to use a low-level access port and to do that, you are going to have to learn how to use the microcontroller; however, it is going to take away from the beauty of the Arduino machine. However, there is going to be a library that you can use to increase the input and output access.

Keep in mind that there are going to be limitations because it is mainly going to support the Leonardo, Mega, Uno, Nana, and Attiny models.

This is going to provide an inline function for faster input-output access.

Analog Readings

Analog readings on a USB powered Arduino model is going to give you some unexpected results. This happens because the analog reference voltage will be tied to the logic voltage which is typically going to be five volts, however, if you are powering your panel from a switch power supply or from the USB you are going to be dealing with commotion and voltage drops because of the USB cable. This is possible as long as your controller is running at four point five instead of five volts.

It is not going to be ideal when it comes to precision measurements. To do the proper measurements, you are going to have to use an external precision voltage reference. On the other hand, you can use the voltage reference that is built into the chip to measure the current VCC and do the calculations that have to be done.

Getting Free RAM

In this section, you are going to learn how to get the free RAM returned in bytes.

Using the Const, Program and Global Variables

In the event that you are having to store a large amount of data in the code that you are using, then you are going to need to make a global const and include the program statement. This is going to tell the program's compiler to store the data in the program memory instead of on the RAM

Forgetting the Default IDE

While the IDE that comes with Arduino is great, it is not going to be suitable for use with professional software development. If you are using it, you are going to realize that it is going to become a pain to use once you have written a program that has more than a few hundred lines.

So, to bypass this, you will use the Atmel Studio or the Visual Studio that comes with the Visual Micro plugin. This plugin is going to have a debugger, but it is vital that you know that it is not free, it is going to cost you seventeen dollars.

You can also use a text editor so that you can write out your programs. However, with Arduino one point five, the IDE is going to support the building and uploading of your program through the command line.

Syntax

Arduino --panel (panel type description) --port (serial port) --upload (sketch path)

Arduino --panel (panel type description) --port (serial port) --verify (sketch path)

You will need to have a panel type description as well.

Syntax

package:arch:panel[:parameters]

You are going to be able to find out more about the command line through the manual documents for Arduino IDE.

Inlining Small Functions

There is a manual that says that the inline function is as fast as a macro. But, there is a catch. If you make an inline function, it is going to make your code size larger; especially if you call the function in several places.

Chapter 11: Arduino function libraries

I/O Function; advanced I/O function; etc.

Functions in Arduino

The Arduino board comes with a number of pins. These pins can be configured to act as either inputs or outputs. It will be good for you to note that most of the Arduino analog pins can be programmed and used in the same way as the digital pins.

INPUT Pins

Pull-up Resistors

Pull-up resistors are used to steer up an input pin to a particular state if no input is available. We can do this by adding a pull-up resistor (to +5V) or a pull-down resistor on the input. You can use a 10K resistor for a pull-up or pull-down resistor.

The Atmega chip has 20,000 pull-up resistors and all can be accessed from the software. To access these built-in pull-up resistors, we set the **pinMode()** to INPUT_PULLUP. This will invert the behavior of the input mode. A value of HIGH will mean that the sensor is ON while a value of LOW will mean that the sensor is OFF. The value of the pull-up will depend on the type of microcontroller that has been used. This value ranges between **20kΩ and 50kΩ on most AVR-based boards. This value ranges between 50kΩ and**

150kΩ on Arduino Due. The exact value is shown ion the datasheet on the microcontroller of the board.

When you connect a sensor to a pin that has been configured with INPUT_PULLUP, you should connect the other end to the ground. If the pin is simple, this will cause the pin to read HIGH when the switch is open and LOW when the pin is pressed. Pull-up resistors can provide enough current to light an LED dimly that has been connected to a pin that has been configured as an input. If you see working LEDs, but lighting dimly, this could be the reason.

The following example demonstrates this:

pinMode($_3$,INPUT) ; //set the pin to input mode without using a built-in pull up resistor

pinMode($_5$,INPUT_PULLUP) ; //set the pin to input using a built-in pull up resistor

Output Pins

A pin that has been configured as OUTPUT using the ***pinMode()*** function is said to be in the ***low-impedance*** state. Such a pin is able to provide a significant amount of current to other circuits.

When you attempt to run high current devices from output pins, you can damage the output transistors in the pin, or destroy the entire Atmega chip. In most cases, this results in a dead pin on the microcontroller but the rest of the chips will function normally.

The **pinMode()** Function

We use this function to configure a particular pin as either an input or an output pin. If you need to enable the internal pull-up resistors, you can use this function with the IINPUT_PULLUP mode. When you use the INPUT mode, it will disable the internal pull-ups.

The **pinMode()** function takes the syntax given below:

Void setup () {

   pinMode (pin, mode);

}

The function takes two parameters as shown in the above syntax. The first parameter is a **pin**, which is the number of the pin whose mode you need to set or modify. The **mode** is the state you want to set the pin to, and it can be **INPUT, OUTPUT, or INPUT_PULLUP.**

Consider the example given below:

int **btn** = 5 ; // The button connected to pin 5

int **LED** = 6; // The LED connected to pin 6

```
void setup () {

    pinMode(btn , INPUT_PULLUP);

    // set the digital pin as input with a pull-up resistor

    pinMode(btn , OUTPUT); // set the digital pin as
output

}

void loop () {

        if (digitalRead(btn ) == LOW){ // if the
        button is pressed
    digitalWrite(LED,HIGH); // turn the led on

        delay(500); // delay for 500 ms
    digitalWrite(LED,LOW); // turn the led off

        delay(500); // a delay of 500 ms
}

}
```

We created two variables, **btn** and **LED**. These denote
the button connected to pin 5 and the LED connected to
pin 6 respectively. Inside the **setup()** function, the
digital pin was set as input with a pull-up resistor. The
digital pin was also set as output.

The logic for the sketch has then been implemented in the *loop()* function. When the button is pressed, the LED will be turned on and delay in the stated for 500 milliseconds. The LED will then turn off and delay in that state for 500 milliseconds.

The digitalWrite( ) Function

We use this function when we need to write a value of HIGH or LOW to a digital pin. If the pin had been configured to be OUTPUT using the *pinMode()* function, it will be assigned a corresponding value of voltage (which is 5V or 3.3V on 3.3V boards) for HIGH, oV (which is ground) for LOW.

If the *pinMode()* function is not set to OUTPUT, then a LED is connected to a pin, a call to *digitalWrite(HIGH)* may make the LED appear dim. If you don't set *pinMode()* explicitly, the *digitalWrite()* function will enable the internal pull-up resistor, which will act like a large resistor resisting the flow of current.

The *digitalWrite()* function takes the following syntax:

```
Void loop() {

   digitalWrite (pin ,value);

}
```

The function takes two arguments, **pin** and **value** as shown in the above syntax. The **pin** denotes the number of the pin whose mode you need to set. The **value** argument can take a value of either HIGH or LOW.

Consider the following example that demonstrates how to use the **digitalWrite()** function:

int **LED** = 6; // A LED connected to pin 6

void setup () {

   pinMode(LED, OUTPUT); // set the digital pin as output

}

void loop () {

   digitalWrite(LED,HIGH); // turn the led on

   delay(500); // delay for 500 ms

   digitalWrite(LED,LOW); // turn the led off

   delay(500); // a delay of 500 ms

}

We created a variable named **LED** to denote the LED that has been connected to pin 6. In the **setup()**

function, this pin was set to act as an output pin. In the **loop()** function, we have used the **digitalWrite()** function to turn the pin on and off. A delay of 500 milliseconds has been added.

The *analogRead()* Function

Arduino whether a voltage has been applied to any of its pins then reports this using the **analogRead()** function. A difference exists between an on/off sensor and an analog sensor. The on/off sensor detects the presence of an object while the value an analogue sensor changes continuously. For us to read an analog sensor, a different type of pin is required.

The lower part of the Arduino board has six pins that have been marked **Analog In.** These pins are able to tell whether a voltage has been applied to them as well as the value of this voltage. The **analogRead()** function can help us read the amount of voltage that has been applied to any of these pins.

The function will always return a value ranging between 0 and 1023, which is a representation of voltage between 0 and 5 volts. For example, if a voltage of 2.5V has been applied to the pin number 0, the **analogRead(0)** will read a value of 512. The 0 passed to the function is the number of the pin. This means that the function takes the number of the pin as the argument as shown in the following syntax:

```
analogRead(pin);
```

The **pin** parameter is the number of analog pins whose value is to be read. Here is an example that demonstrates how to use the **analogRead()** function in Arduino:

```
int analogPin = 3;// a potentiometer wiper
   // connected to the analog pin 3
int x = 0; // variable to store the read value

void setup() {
   Serial.begin(9600); // setup serial
}

void loop() {
   x = analogRead(analogPin); // to read the input pin
   Serial.println(x); // print the value
}
```

We began by creating a variable named *analogRead* and assigning it a value of 3. This variable denotes a potentiometer wiper that has been connected to the analog pin number 3. We have also created a second variable, *x*, and assigned it a value of 0. We will use this variable to store the value that has been read from the pin, which is the voltage applied to the pin. In the *loop()* function, we have called the *analogRead()* function and passed the value *analogPin* to it as the parameter. This will read the value of the voltage on the analog pin number 3 and store the read value in the variable *x*. We have then printed out this value.

The analogReference() Function

This function configures the reference voltage that is used for analog input, that is, the value that has been used as the top of the input range. The function can take any of the following options:

DEFAULT – This is the default analog reference of 5 volts on the 5V Arduino boards or 3.3 volts on the 3.3V Arduino boards.

INTERNAL – This is a built-in reference, which is equal to 1.1 volts on ATmega168 or the ATmega328 and 2.56 volts on ATmega8. It is not available on the Arduino Mega.

INTERNAL1V1 – This is a built-in 1.1V reference. It is available on Arduino Mega only.

INTERNAL2V56 – This is a built-in 2.56V reference. It is available on Arduino Mega only.

EXTERNAL – This is the voltage applied to the AREF pin, that is, 0 to 5V only, and it is used as the reference.

The function takes the following syntax:

analogReference (type);

The parameter **type** can be any of the options discussed above.

Avoid using anything that is less than 0V or above 5V for external reference voltage on the AREF pin. In case you are using an external reference on the AREF pin, you should set the analog reference to EXTERNAL before you can call the **analogRead()** function. If you don't do this, you will short the active reference voltage, which is generated internally, and the AREF pin, which may damage the microcontroller on your Arduino board.

You can also connect the external reference voltage to the AREF pin via a 5K resistor, which will allow you to switch between the internal and external reference voltages. The resistor will change the voltage that has been used as the reference since the AREF pin has an internal 32K resistor. The two will act as a voltage divider.

The following example demonstrates how to use the *analogReference()* function:

```
int analogPin = 3;// a potentiometer wiper connected
to analog pin 3

int x = 0; // a variable for storing the read value


void setup() {

    Serial.begin(9600); // to setup serial

    analogReference(EXTERNAL); // voltage applied to
AREF pin

        // is used as the reference.

}


void loop() {

    x = analogRead(analogPin); // to read the input
pin

    Serial.println(x); // to print the value

}
```

We began by creating a variable named **analogRead** and assigning it a value of 3. This variable denotes a potentiometer wiper that has been connected to the analog pin number 3. We have also created a second variable, **x**, and assigned it a value of 0. We will use this variable to store the value that has been read from the pin, which is the voltage applied to the pin.

Consider the following line extracted from the code:

analogReference**(EXTERNAL);**

This line simply means that the voltage that is applied to the AREF pin, which ranges between 0 and 5V, will be used as the reference.

In the **loop()** function, we have called the **analogRead()** function and passed the value **analogPin** to it as the parameter. This will read the value of the voltage on the analog pin number 3 and store the read value in the variable **x**. We have then printed out this value.

Character Functions

We enter data into a computer in the form of **characters**. The characters can be **letters, digits and other special symbols.**

The library for handling characters comes with a number of functions that we can use to test and manipulate characters of data. Every function receives data in the form of int, or EOF as an argument. This means that the characters are manipulated as integers.

The EOF usually has a value of -1 and some hardware architectures don't allow for the storage of negative values as char variables. This means that the functions for handling characters manipulate them as strings.

Anytime we need to use the functions for handling characters, we should add the <cctype> header to the program. The following the different functions provided by the character-handling library:

The **isdigit** function checks whether its argument is a digit or not. The **isalpha** function determines whether the argument passed to it is an uppercase letter, that is, A-Z, or lowercase letter, that is, a-z. The **isalnum** function checks whether the argument passed to it is an uppercase letter, a lowercase letter or a digit. The **isxdigit** function checks whether the argument passed to it is a hexadecimal digit, that is, A-F, a-f or 0-9.

The conditional operator (?:) can be used with every function to determine whether the string " is a" or " is not a" should be printed in the output of every character that has been tested

We now need to create an example that demonstrates how to use the **isupper** and the **islower** functions. We use the ***isupper*** function to check whether the argument passed to it is uppercase, that is, A-Z. We use the ***islower*** function to check whether the argument passed to it is lower, that is, a-z.

The code will return the following when executed:

The islower function returns:

m is a lowercase letter

M is <u>not</u> a lowercase letter

6 is <u>not</u> a lowercase letter

! is <u>not</u> a lowercase letter

The isupper function returns:

D is an uppercase letter

d is <u>not</u> an uppercase letter

9 is <u>not</u> an uppercase letter

$ is <u>not</u> an uppercase letter

We now need to create an example that demonstrates the use of ***isdigit, isalpha, isalnum*** and ***isxdigit*** functions. The ***isdigit*** function helps us check whether the argument passed to it is a digit, that is, 0-9. The ***isalph*** function helps us check whether the argument passed to it is an uppercase letter, that is, A-Z, or a lowercase letter, that is, a-z. The *isalnum* function determines whether the argument passed to it is a lowercase, uppercase letter or a digit. The *isxdigit* function checks whether the argument passed to it is a hexadecimal digit, that is, a-f, A-F, or 0-9.

Conditional Operator

The conditional operator (?:) is used with every function to determine whether the string "is a" or "is not a" should be printed in the output of every character that is tested.

We now need to create an example that demonstrates how to use the *islower* and the *isupper* functions. The *islower* function checks whether the argument passed to it is a lowercase letter, that is, a-z. The *isupper* function checks whether the argument passed to it is uppercase, that is, A-Z.

Chapter 12: Computer interfacing with an Arduino

The FTDI Chips; Example of Temperature sensors with serial interface

Before you begin to program your Arduino, you will need to understand the basic sketch of a microcontroller. A sketch is the term used to describe an Arduino program. It is the code uploaded to an Arduino board, where it then runs to allow the microcontroller to perform specific functions. Now that you know what a sketch is, you should be able to comprehend how they work with Arduino commands. The most basic commands of Arduino involve the digital and analog pins. We will discuss these in this chapter. However, remember that these are only a small amount of the commands that you can complete using the Arduino board. These commands are used in conjunction with input and output values to write codes. Arduino codes can be long and complex. Many of them are found in the Arduino library. The flexibility of the program even allows you to write your own coding in the event that you cannot find coding to make your project perform the function that you want it to.

Basic Commands

The basic Arduino commands include BareMinimum, Fade, Blink, ReadAnalogVoltage, AnalogReadSerial, and DigitalReadSerial.

BareMinimum: The least amount of coding needed to run an Arduino sketch. Two command lines are used with this. **Void setup( )** and **void loop ( ).** The setup function runs once each time the board is started and once when the board is reset. The loop function is used to allow your program to respond and change to your commands.

Fade: This command is used with an analog output to fade an LED light on your Arduino board.

Blink: The blink command will make an LED turn on and off.

ReadAnalogVoltage: This command will allow the microcontroller to read an analog input, before printing the voltage onto the serial monitor of the Arduino.

AnalogReadSerial: This command is responsible for reading a potentiometer. It can then print the state of the potentiometer to a serial monitor.

DigitalReadSerial: This command lets the Arduino read a switch. Then, the Arduino will make this visible by printing the state to a serial monitor.

Analog

The analog commands are designed to work specifically with the analog inputs and outputs on the Arduino board. These include Analog Input, AnalogInOutSerial, Calabration, AnalogWriteMega, Smoothing, and Fading.

Analog Input: This command is used with a potentiometer to cause an LED to blink on and off as needed.

AnalogInOutSerial: This command works by first reading an analog input pin. Then, AnalogInOutSerial maps the result of the input pin and uses those results to cause an LED light to either brighten or dim.

Calibration: This command is used to define expected values for an analog sensor using a minimum and maximum value.

AnalogWriteMega: This command is designed to work with the Arduino Mega microcontroller. It sequentially fades 12 separate LEDs on and off.

Smoothing: The smoothing command is used to smooth analog input readings if there are several of them.

Fading: As the command name suggests, the fading command is responsible for causing an LED to fade. It does this using a PWM pin.

Digital

The digital functions can play musical tones, control the function of LEDs, and read pushbuttons. These functions include Simple Keyboard, Tone, Tone4, Pitch Follower, Debounce, Button State Change, Button, and Blink Without Delay.

Simple Keyboard: This turns your Arduino into a musical keyboard with three keys by using a pizo speaker and force sensors.

Tone: This command is to be used in conjunction with a Piezo speaker to play a melody.

Tone4: This uses the tone command with multiple speakers to play sequential tones.

Pitch Follower: This uses an analog input and a Piezo speaker to play a certain pitch.

Debounce: This command is used to filter noise by reading a pushbutton that has been linked to your Arduino.

Button State Change: This command allows your Arduino to count the number of times a button has been pressed.

Button: The button command allows your Arduino to control an LED when an attached pushbutton is pressed.

Blink Without Delay: This command allows an LED on your board to blink without the delay function, meaning it can blink faster or remain constantly lit.

Chapter 13: C language Basics

The Memory Maps

When you create an Arduino program, it is essential to have some knowledge about the working of computer systems. Even though C programming is the language that is close to the machines, how certain things are done when the program runs will become clear.

A primary system consists of the control device referred to as the CPU or microcontroller. There are a few differences when it comes to some of these. We shall dig deep into this later. Just to mention, microcontrollers may not be that powerful compared to the standard microprocessor. However, it still contains input, output ports, as well as hardware functions.

Microprocessors are connected to the external Memory. Generally, microcontrollers contain a sufficient amount of onboard memory. However, it should be noted that we are not referring to the large sizes; it is possible for a microcontroller to have only a few hundred bytes or so of memory for the simple applications. Don't forget that a memory byte has 8 bits, and each bit can either be true or false, high or low and I/ O.

When it comes to the relation between the processor and the functional data stored in the memory, data must be kept in the processor's register. The register is the only place where we can have logical mathematical operations carried out. For example, if you would like to carry out an addition of two variables, the value of the variables has to be moved over to the register.

Memory Maps

Each memory byte in the computer system has a connected address. Now, if we do not have the address, the processor will not have a means to identify a particular memory. In general, the memory address begins from 0 as it increases. Even though we have specific addresses with a private or unique system, a particular address may not point to the input and output port of external communication.

Most of the time, you will find it necessary to map-out the memory. This is merely a massive array of memory slots. We have people who develop a memory map and have the address with the least value positioned at the top while others who draw a memory map and assign the least address at the bottom. Each address points to a place where it can have the byte stored. However, the C compiler will complete this. For instance, if we declare the char variable as –X. It can be located at address 2, so if we print the value, there would be no need to select the value at the address 2. We will instead write, "select the X value" where the compiler produces code to ensure that it works correctly to the right address. Using this level of abstraction simplifies the whole process. However, since most variables carry a specific amount that is higher than one byte, we might have to collect these addresses to hold only a single value. For example, if we pick a short int, then it will require us to have two bytes. Now, if the following address starts at four, there is a need to use the address 5. When we choose to access this particular variable, the compiler will automatically build the code and make use of all the addresses since it is aware of the presence of the short int.

Stacks

Most programmers prefer to use temporary storages for the variables. What this means is that there are variables that are used for a short period then they are discarded. Therefore, it will not be right if we move on and allocate a permanent space for this particular variable. Ordinarily, an application is made up of two parts: the code and the data. The data part is permanent since these two parts cannot consume the whole memory; the remaining memory is used temporarily for storage via the stack. It starts at the opposite end of the memory map; the stack increases towards the data part as well as the code. It is similar to the stack of trays. The first tray on the stack will be the last to be pulled off. Any time temporary variables are needed, this part of the memory is used. Given that many items are required, most of the memory will be used up. When the code ends, the temporary variables declared are no longer useful, and therefore the stack shrinks.

The Basics of C-language

C language is designed for professional developers who want to accomplish many things with less code. C is a compiler language. This shows that once we have written the program, we must transfer it into the compiler that will begin to change the C language instructions into a machine code that the microcontroller can manage.

As you can see, this is an additional step to take, but it will result in a better program compared to the interpreter. After this, the interpreter will convert the code from the machine language.

It is crucial for the machine to have an interpreter. You can look at it as a compiler that translates it once instead of line-by-line.

However, C is not the same as in other languages. It is a free-flow language. We have the statements, functions, and variables. Variables, as we have already seen, are objects that can store things. It can be a floating-point number or other types of variables. Statements have assignments, operations and so on.

Functions have statements and can call other functions.

How to name variables, and declare

The naming of variables in C is quite easy. Names of variables carry with them numerals, underscores, and letters. You can as well combine the upper and lower case. However, the length cannot go past the 31 characters. However, the actual limit depends on the C compiler. In addition, variables cannot contain reserved keywords or unique characters like a semicolon, comma, and other special characters. Therefore, valid names can be names such as resistor8, volt5, and we_are_variables. C language has different variable types. Some of them consist of floating-point numbers and real numbers in two forms. First, there is the 32-bit float, and then the double. We also have a few types of integers that consist of char, 16 bits, short int, and 32 bits long int. Though char is only an 8 bit, still has a 2 to the 8th combinations – or even 256 separate values that you will find it perfect for a single ASCII character. Similar to other languages, the C language has arrays and compound data types. When it comes to variables in the C language, it is vital for the variables to be declared before they are used. Variables cannot just be created instantly like the way it happens in the Python language. Variable declarations are made up of the variable type and variable name. You can also include an initial value for the variable during the declaration, but that is optional. Multiple variable declarations are still allowed in C language. For instance:

Float c = 1.2;

Char c;

Unsigned char x;

You should underline that every type of variable declaration ends with a semi-colon. Like many other programming languages such as Java, the semi-colon indicates the end of that statement.

Functions

Functions have a similar naming rule like variables. All functions have a similar syntax that resembles: Return_value function_name (function argument list) { Statement(s) } You can borrow the concept of mathematical functions where you assign it some value(s) as well as allocate back some values. An example is a calculator that contains the cosine function. It is possible to assign an angle to it, and this will return a specific value. Functions may contain separate arguments in the C language. Furthermore, it is possible for a C function to return values. A void function is one that does not require a value or return a value. A void function will look like this:

void function_name (void)

{

// necessary statements come here

}

This might look like a lot of work, but the data types in the C language make sense. What this means is that if you choose to use a wrong kind of variable in a function, or even an incorrect number of variables, you will receive a warning.

Therefore, if you have a float function and attempt to send it an integer variable, the compiler will send you a warning. Every program must have a start and an end. In the C language, all programs begin at the main function. You can look at the program below:

```
void main (void)

{

float y = 3.0;

float f = 2.0;

float t;

t = y* t

}
```

There exists one main() function. It accepts no variables and returns nothing.

Libraries

The previous example is limited because it is hard to see the result. Therefore, you will need some methods when you want to display the results on your computer screen. To achieve this, it will depend on the libraries and systems functions. Countless libraries have the most advanced C systems. In essence, somebody has just tested, compiled and wrote a collection of functions. What you need to do is to link the functions into the program. Linking helps integrate the code and any existing library into an entire program. To display the general data and the input data, we use the standard IO and the stdio.

The stdio library has a function called printf().

The program will display the words "Hello World" on the computer screen. It will further insert a new line after the backslash-n combo. The \n refers to the addition of a new line. If we failed to include the #include directive, the compiler will not understand anything concerning the printf(), and it would show up an error when we attempt to use it. Well,what about the header file? The header file has a lot of different function prototypes. These prototypes can be seen as templates but if you want, you can build your own. To make use of it, you are required to have the correct include statement written into the code, and it will be better set if you remember to include the linker library code. This will not only save time but also allow you to reuse the code.

Simple Math

C has certain basic math operators just like other languages. Some of them include the -, +, / and the multiple. Parentheses help divide the elements and power hierarchy operations. The C language has the % operator that represents modulo. The modulo is an operation which carries the remainders of a division. For example, 8 modulo 18 would, of course, be 2. The division will behave separately both to integers and floats which have no remainder. In other words, integer 5 divided by 2 is 2, and not 2.5. Within the C language, there is a sequence of bit manipulators useful for situations such as this. For complex math operators, you will have to go deep into the math library. Some of the examples are log (10), tan(), cos() and sin().

However, you should not attempt to use the ^ operator because it has a separate meaning in the C language. Well, do you still remember what we said earlier about the use of libraries? Placing certain functions such as sin() into your code forces the compiler to define the prototypes along with other related information. Therefore, during the start of the program, it will be necessary to include the following line:

#include < math.h >

C Language Input and Output

We know that the prinf() function displays the information on the screen. The printf() is an extensive and complex function which has a lot of variants and format specifiers. The format specifiers comprise of the % stuff applied as the placeholders for the values.

Take for instance, if we want to show the value of a variable in the decimal form. We could have done it this way: printf (" The value is %d, in hex %x, and in octal is &o.\ n", value1, value1, value1); You should see the way we have labeled the variables. This is critical because if you make a mistake and display a value that has no label, it will be impossible to tell whether it is a hex or decimal. For instance, if you see a number like 22, how will you tell that the number is a decimal or hex for that matter? It is impossible to know.

Besides indicating the label, you can print it with a field width. For instance, %6d is equivalent to writing the integer in the decimal with a minimum space of 6. Similarly, %6.2f implies that you print the floating-point value with a minimum of 6 spaces. The .2 part is an exact specifier, and in the following example, it shows two digits after the decimal point. You can then see how powerful and flexible this function looks. The input function for the C language is the scanf(). This resembles the Python's input statement. Even though it is possible to request different values at once, it is the best.

It comes with similar specifiers like the printf(). So, there is a point which needs to be understood, and the scanf() function will require you to specify the location where the value is kept in the computer memory. This shows that just writing the name of the variable is not enough. You need to describe it in detail. C has the & operator which means the address of. For example, when you want to select a specific integer variable from a user and store it snugly inside the voltage variable. Here is the code fragment for you to look at:

printf (" Kindly type in the voltage"); scanf ("% d," &voltage);

There are hundreds of communication procedures that are defined by Arduino and will be used to achieve the data exchange. Every procedure is going to will be placed into one of two categories, serial or parallel.

Parallel

A parallel connection between the peripherals and Arduino will be established through input and output ports so that there is a shorter distance of several meters. But, in some cases, it is going to be required that communication is established between two pieces of equipment over a longer distance, and you are not going to be able to use parallel connections. Parallel interfaces will move a group of bits at the same time. They will typically require a bus of data that are going to transmit through the wires labeled eight and sixteen. The data transfer is going to be massive.

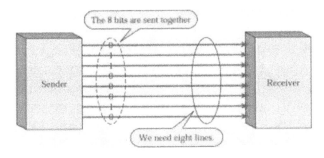

Pros and Cons

While parallel communication is going to have its advantages, such as it is faster and more straightforward as well as easier to implement. However, it is going to require a lot of input and output lines and ports. If you find that you need to move a project from an Uno panel to a Mega board, you are going to have to know the input-output lines on the microprocessor, and you will be aware that there are not going to be many. So, you are going to discover you like to use serial communication which means that you are going to be sacrificing the potential speed for pin real estate.

Serial Communication

In most panels that you are going to use today, there are several systems that are built in for serial communication.

The system that is used will be determined by the following factors:

1.   Do you need to be able to send and receive data simultaneously?
2.   How many pieces of equipment is the microcontroller exchanging data with?
3.   What is the space between the pieces of equipment?
4.   How fast does the data transfer need to be?
It is of vital importance to establish procedure whenever you are working with serial communication. The procedure is going to have to be strictly observed. This set of rules is going to be applied so that the device knows how to interpret the data that is being exchanged. Thankfully, Arduino is going to automatically take care of this so that the user is dealing with clear data.

Types of Serial Communication

1. **Asynchronous: a device that is asynchronous is going to have its own clock that will be triggered by an output of the previous state.**

2. Synchronous: for a device that is synchronized with another, it is going to be using the same clock, and the timing is going to be synchronized with each other.

It is going to be easy to discover if the device you are using is synchronous or not. Should the same clock be given to all the pieces of equipment that are connected, then they are going synchronous. However, if there is no clock line, it is going to be asynchronous.

An example would be the UART – universal asynchronous receiver transmitter – module will be asynchronous.

The asynchronous procedure is going to have several rules built in. these rules are not going to be anymore more than mechanisms that are going to help to ensure data transfers are robust and error-free. The mechanisms are going to be:

1. **Baud rate**

2. Synchronization bits

3. **Parity bits**

4. Data Bits

Synchronized Bits

Synchronized bits are two or three bits that are special and will be transferred with every packet of data. They are going to be bits designated for starting and stopping the sending of data packets. Just like their name suggests, these bits will mark the beginning and the end of a packet.

There is always going to be a single start bit, but there can be multiple stop bits that can be configured to each other.

Your start bit will always be indicated by an idle data line that is going to go from one to zero while the stop bits are going to transition to idle holding the line at one.

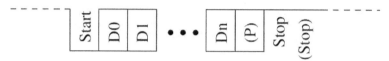

Data Bits

The magnitude of data that is in each package will have the option of being set five to nine bits. The standard size is going to be eight bits; however, the other bit sizes are going to have their uses. Like a seven-bit packet is going to be more efficient than an eight bit if you are transferring seven-bit ASCII characters.

Parity bits

You are going to have the option of picking whether there should be a parity bit or not and if they decide there should be, then the parity bit is going to be odd or even. The parity bit will be zero in the event that the digital representation of ones inside the data bit is even, then the odd parity will be labeled as the opposite.

Baud rate

This function is going to be used to denote the digital representation of bits that are being transferred per second. Keep in mind that this is going to refer to bits and not bytes. The baud rate will typically be required by the procedure that each byte is transferred along with several control bits. That means that for every one byte there will be eleven bits.

Uart

Once the sketch has been uploaded to Arduino, you are going to have to open serial monitor which is located at the top right of the IDE.

You can type in whatever you want in the top box of the serial monitor and press send. This is going to send a series of bytes to the Arduino panel that you are using.

The code will return whatever is received as an input.

Chapter 14: Arduino clones and similar boards

The Microcontroller/ Main Chip

This is the brain of the Arduino board. This is the part which is programmed. It is the one responsible for running the code, hence it can be seen as the CPU (Central Processing Board) of the board.

This chip has some legs, which are usually plugged into the socket. These can be seen once it is taken out of the socket. However, they are not referred to as "legs" but "pins".

Power Jack and Supply

There are two ways on how you can supply power to your Arduino board. You may choose to use a USB connector to establish a connection to a computer or some portable power jack, or you may choose to plug it to the wall adapter. The USB can be used for powering and programming. The DC is only used for powering the board, and it is the best if you are in need of connecting the board and leaving it for some long-term project.

USB Jack and Interface

The USB Jack is the cable that helps you connect your board to the computer. You can use any computer, provided it has a USB port.

Some processor chips will fail when you are using a USB cable for connection to a computer. In such a case, you will have to use the serial interface. You must have a USB to the serial interface translator chip.

The LEDs

The Arduino comes with some lights from which you can draw ideas regarding what it is up to. The lights are referred to as LEDs. The Arduino board comes with 4 LEDs which are *L*, *RX*, *TX*, and *ON.* On the UNO board, you will find three of these at the center and one on the right side.

The ON LED will turn to green once you have powered the Arduino board. In case you find it off or flickering, then just check on your power connection.

The RX and TX boards will blink whenever data is being sent from the board or being received on the board. The TX LED will light yellow once you send data from Arduino to the computer USB port. The RX LED will light yellow whenever data is sent to Arduino from the computer's USB port.

The LED is the one that you are able to control. The other 3 LEDS usually light automatically. The L LED has been connected to the main chip of the Arduino. This can be turned on and off once you begin to write the code.

Headers

This is the main part of the Arduino board. These are the two lines of sockets that line up with edges of the circuit board. The thin sockets will allow you to plugin some wires into them. The wires can, in turn, be connected to any types of electronic parts including sensors, LEDs, displays, motors etc.

USB Fuse

The little USB fuse protects the computer and the Arduino. There are high chances that all types of wires will be connected to the Arduino, which may cause an accidental short on the wires. The importance of this fuse comes during this time. It is resettable, and in such occurrence, it will just open up in the same way a fuse or circuit breaker works. This will protect your board from damage.

Reset Button

This button is located next to the USB jack. However, on some other boards, you may find it on the right side. It is the button that can be used for restarting the Arduino. Restarting the board will only take a second, and it is done if it gets stuck or if you need to re-run some program.

Power up Test

We are now ready to power on our Arduino board. You can simply do this by connecting one end of your USB cable to the Arduino board and the other one to your computer. The computer will act as the source of power for the Arduino.

If you are using Arduino UNO, then the USB cable should have its end as square B-type. The USB cable should be plugged directly to the computer port. After you are sure that you are able to power the Arduino then upload the sketches, you will be set. You can then plug it to the other ports. For you to know whether the power source is working correctly, just check on whether the ON LED is lit green. The L or yellow LED may also blink or light up, which the same case with the RX and TX LEDs.

Chapter 15: Troubleshooting

Arduino Board Testing

In the process of circuit building, there will come a time when nothing will be working. This moment will call for a process of troubleshooting and debugging in order to identify and solve the problems with your experiment.

Key points to a successful troubleshooting:

Understanding: Always ensure that you properly understand all the components used in your experiment. Clearly mark out the power flow all these components are connected with one another.

Simplification and Segmentation: This is more like divide and rule tactic where you break down the project and figure out the problem with each and every component

Exclusion and Certainty: This involves investing each part separately and being sure of their functionality. Through this you will be able ascertain the problem with each component.

Board testing therefore involves "Blinking an LED", if it does not work, check on the USB connection and other more options explored below.

Breadboard Circuit Testing

Run a short circuit test by connecting your Arduino board to the breadboard. If the PWR LED turns OFF then there is a serious short circuit connection on your board. Quickly begin segmentation and simplification to find the wrong connection.

Problem Identification

Some of the common problems with Arduino programming are listed below:

☐ Arduino IDE not launching: Use the **run.bat** files as alternative option.

☐ Windows Operating System assigning a COM port which is greater to Arduino: Solve this by convincing windows to assign a lower COM port. For other versions of Windows, follow the procedures described earlier in this book about **Port Identification**.

Problem Isolation and Solving

This option provides for you to reproduce a problem. When your circuit exhibits some problems, find out the exact place and place (component) associated with that particular problem. This will help you to correctly describe a problem and possibly suggest a solution.

Online Help

In case the above suggestions do no work, you are welcomed to seek online help on the Arduino website:

www. Arduino.cc/en/Guide. While seeking online help, be sure to specify the following parameters:

☐   The type of Arduino board you are using.

☐   The Operating System you are using to run Arduino IDE.

☐   Give a general description of your problem.

☐   Of course use CAPITALS to specify all these.

CONCLUSION

This marks the end of this book. You can program the Arduino board so as to come up with complex systems. An example of such a system is one that controls access to a facility. You can use Arduino to program the door that grants access to the facility. Arduino is good for hardware programming. If you are familiar with the C programming language, then it is easy for you to program the Arduino boards. The code is written in the Arduino software, which is an open source software. You can download and use this software on your system or free. The codes written in the Arduino software are known as sketches. There are a number of libraries that you need to include in your programs when programming the Arduino board. These libraries are included by the use of the "#include" keyword used in the C programming language. You can write programs that can control the Arduino LED light. Note that you can power the Arduino board from your computer or directly into the power socket, and the effect will be the same in all of these cases. Data can be sent from the computer to the Arduino board, and from the Arduino board to the computer. The RX and TX LEDs usually light to show the direction in which the data is flowing.

When programming the Arduino board, you can take advantage of the various features provided by the language including decision making statements, loops, functions, variables and others. The language also supports various data types that you can use when declaring variables. The **math.h** library comes with a number of functions that you can to perform various mathematical operations. An example of such a function is the **sqrt()** function that can help you calculate the square root of a number.